The Messiah before Jesus

The *Messiah* before Jesus

The Suffering Servant of the Dead Sea Scrolls

ISRAEL KNOHL

Translated by David Maisel

UNIVERSITY OF CALIFORNIA PRESS

Berkeley   Los Angeles   London

*The publisher gratefully acknowledges the
generous contribution to this book provided by
Jack Miles and also by the S. Mark Taper foundation.*

University of California Press

Berkeley and Los Angeles, California

University of California Press, Ltd.

London, England

© 2000 by the Regents of the University of California

Library of Congress Cataloging-in-Publication Data

Knohl, Israel.
    The Messiah before Jesus : the suffering servant of
the Dead Sea scrolls / Israel Knohl ; translated by
David Maisel.
        p.   cm.
    Includes bibliographical references and index.
    ISBN 0-520-21592-3 (cloth : alk. paper)
        1. Dead Sea scrolls—Criticism, interpretation,
etc.   2. Dead Sea scrolls—Relation to the New Testament.   3. Jesus Christ—Messiahship.   4. Servant
of Jehovah.   5. Christianity—Origin.   I. Title.
BM487 .K63 2000
296.3'36—dc21   00-037404
                                                        CIP

Manufactured in the United States of America

09   08   07   06   05   04   03   02   01   00

10   9   8   7   6   5   4   3   2   1

The paper used in this publication meets the minimum
requirements of ANSI/NISO Z39.48-1992 (R 1997)
(*Permanence of Paper*). ∞

For my wife, Rivka, and for our children,
Shay, Tal, and Or

CONTENTS

FIGURES

PREFACE

"Knohl is a lonely figure, swimming against the tide of one hundred years of scholarship."[1]

This is how one scholar described my study of priestly literature in my first book, *The Sanctuary of Silence*. In that work I questioned a theory about the composition of the Pentateuch that had been accepted by Bible scholars for more than a century. Ten years later I find myself in a similar situation. In the present work I challenge the point of view dominant in New Testament scholarship for over a hundred years. My personal feelings also resemble those of ten years ago: concern on the one hand, and on the other, a strong compulsion to reveal the truth as I see it.

The great difference in this case is the degree of public interest in the subject in question. My first book dealt with matters chiefly of interest to scholars, and I therefore adopted an academic style suited to a work addressed to professionals. The present work, however, concerns the messianic figure of Jesus, a subject of interest to numerous people throughout the world.

For this reason I decided to write the book in a way that would be easy to read and comprehensible to the general public. This necessitated a simplification of the text. Elucidation of the more complex textual and historical questions was therefore transferred to the notes and appendices. In order to enable the general reader to enter into the atmosphere of the period treated in the book, I begin the work with an imaginary description of a day in the life of the Messiah. I trust that scholars will also find this description of interest and will not judge it with academic severity.

Finally, I wish to say a few words about the Dead Sea Scrolls, on which the main argument of the book is based. In recent years, some have claimed that there has been a deliberate delay in publishing the scrolls because of pressures from the Vatican and other quarters. The argument is that the Vatican wishes to delay publication of parts of the scrolls for fear that the material they contain might be prejudicial to the uniqueness of the figure of Jesus. On the face of it, my book might seem to provide evidence in support of this claim; for on the basis of some fragments published in recent years I try to demonstrate that Jesus was regarded as heir and successor to the Messiah described in the Dead Sea Scrolls. I therefore wish to make it quite clear that I find the charge of a deliberate delay in publishing the scrolls unacceptable. As someone personally involved in the publication of several fragments of the scrolls, I know how much painstaking labor goes into the publication of each individual fragment in a responsible manner.

I have the highest regard for the scholars involved in the publication of the fragments discussed in this book, namely, M. Baillet, J. J. Collins, D. Dimant, E. Eshel, J. T. Milik, E. Puech, and E. Schuller. Even if my views sometimes differ from theirs, I realize this book could never have been written without the firm basis they have so competently provided.

I began the research for this book in March 1997. My first article on the subject was published in the Hebrew daily magazine *Ha'aretz* on 10 June 1997. I also lectured on "The Messiah of Qumran" at the International Congress on the Dead Sea Scrolls that took place in Jerusalem in the summer of 1997. I did not know at the time that another scholar, Michael O. Wise, was working on a similar subject. His book, *The First Messiah*, was published in 1999. The reader will immediately see, however, that despite the external similarity, my thesis is completely different from his, since we discuss different messianic figures who lived at different times.

In the course of my search for the Messiah of the Dead Sea Scrolls, I was encouraged and assisted by friends. While writing the book I enjoyed the advice of Professor Moshe Idel and Dr. Shlomo Naeh, my colleagues at the Institute of Jewish Studies of the Hebrew University and the Shalom Hartman Institute.

Professor Emmanuel Tov, my colleague in the Department of Bible at the Hebrew University and editor-in-chief of the Qumran Publication Project, carefully read the manuscript and made detailed and valuable suggestions.

Mr. David Maisel made a skillful and faithful translation of the Hebrew manuscript into English.

Doug Abrams Arava, Scott Norton, and Malcolm Reed, my editors at the University of California Press, gave me much help in producing a book suitable for the general public. Carolyn Bond did an excellent job in her careful and skillful editing of my manuscript.

The Shalom Hartman Institute and its director, Professor David Hartman, provided me with excellent working conditions. My heartfelt thanks are due to all of them.

Finally, I would like to thank my wife, Rivka. Without her support and encouragement this book could not have been written.

Israel Knohl
Department of Bible
Hebrew University
Jerusalem

Introduction

To understand Christianity and its relationship to Judaism one must answer a profound and difficult question: What was the Jewish context of Jesus' messianic career? With the discovery of the Dead Sea Scrolls there was great anticipation that the elusive answer to this question might be found within them. However, this hope has not been realized. While parallel language has been noted between the Dead Sea Scrolls and the New Testament, no direct connection to Jesus has been found—until, I believe, now.

The nature of Jesus' messiahship as described in the New Testament has remained a puzzle for almost two thousand years. According to the Synoptic Gospels, Jesus never declared himself to be the Messiah.[1] Moreover, when others called him the Messiah, he asked that it not be publicly revealed.[2] Jesus is represented as often foretelling the rejection, death, and resurrection of the "son of man,"[3] but he never spoke in the first person in this context. In the Gospel of John and in the writings of Paul, Jesus is depicted as a Messiah of divine character who brings redemption and absolution to the world. In contrast, the Jesus of the Synoptic Gospels is a human figure distinguished for his miraculous deeds.

How can we solve the riddle of Jesus' personality and messianic self-understanding? Did he regard himself as the Messiah? If so, why did he not say so plainly, and why did he forbid his disciples to make his messianic identity known to the public, thus creating a "messianic secret"? Did Jesus really foresee his own suffering, death, and resurrection? If he did, why did he not refer to himself directly in this context, but only indirectly, as the "son of man"? Did Jesus see himself as a divine redeemer? If so, why is this not reflected in the Synoptic Gospels?

The main tendency in New Testament scholarship for over a hundred years has been to attempt to resolve these difficulties by denying the historical reality of Jesus' claim to messiahship.[4] Scholars of this viewpoint maintain that Jesus did not regard himself as a Messiah at all and that he was proclaimed Messiah by his disciples only after his death.[5] Jesus, they claim, could not have foreseen his rejection, death, and resurrection, as "the idea of a suffering, dying, and rising Messiah or son of Man was unknown to Judaism."[6] It follows that in the opinion of these scholars, all accounts of Jesus foretelling his rejection, death, and resurrection lack any historical basis whatsoever.[7] These things, they assert, were only ascribed to him after his death.[8]

In this book I intend to counter these claims. I propose to show that Jesus really did regard himself as the Messiah and truly expected the Messiah to be rejected, killed, and resurrected after three days, for this is precisely what was believed to have happened to a messianic leader who had lived one generation before Jesus.

In certain hymns that were found among the Dead Sea Scrolls and have recently been published, this earlier Messiah described himself as sitting on a heavenly throne, surrounded by angels. He regarded himself as the "suffering servant" who brought in a new age, an age of redemption and absolution in which there was no sin or guilt. These audacious ideas led to his rejection and excommunication by the Pharisee sages under the leadership of Hillel.

This Messiah was finally killed in Jerusalem, and his body was left in the street for three days. His disciples believed that he had arisen after three days and had ascended to heaven. The humiliation, rejection, and slaying of the Messiah caused a crisis of faith among his followers. In order to come to terms with this crisis, they sought passages in the Bible that could be understood as prophecies of the humiliation and death of the Messiah. Thus, for the first time in the history of Judaism, a conception emerged of "catastrophic" messianism in which the humiliation, rejection, and death of the Messiah were regarded as an inseparable part of the redemptive process.

The hero of our book, this slain Messiah, is the missing link in our understanding of the way Christianity emerged from Judaism. Jesus was born about the time this Messiah died. Jesus' messianic personality becomes clearer when set in relation to the life and death of this Messiah. A reconstruction of the story of the murdered Messiah allows us for the first time to provide historical background for the account of Jesus' messianic awareness in the New Testament. We are now able to grasp the struggle that waged in Jesus' soul between his natural desire to live and the messianic vocation of rejection, suffering, and death, which he had inherited from his predecessor, the "suffering servant" of the Dead Sea Scrolls.

CHAPTER ONE

The Messianic Secret

A DAY IN THE LIFE OF THE MESSIAH

The time: A day in January in the year 18 BCE.

The place: Jerusalem, Herod's palace, in the western part of the Upper City,[1] and the Essene Quarter of Jerusalem, to the south of the palace.[2]

The Messiah gets up early in the morning, before the sun rises,[3] and goes to the "House of Prostration,"[4] the Essenes' place of assembly and prayer in Jerusalem. In this building, high up on a hill, all the members of the community have gathered for morning prayers.[5] After prayers the Messiah leaves the building. The winter sun rises in the east over the Dead Sea and the Mountains of Moab, which are visible in the distance. The Messiah walks in a northerly direction, leaving the houses of the Essene Quarter, and soon reaches King Herod's palace.

The luxurious palace, which has been completed only recently,[6] is surrounded by a high wall and is protected on the northern side by three enormous towers. The palace consists of two large and splendid buildings: one is called the "Caesareon," after the Roman emperor Augustus, and the other the "Agrippeon," after Agrippa, Augustus's son-in-law, with whom Herod enjoys friendly relations.[7] In the courtyard of the palace are porticoes and a garden filled with trees, pools of water, and bronze fountains.[8] There are also many dovecotes, as the king is fond of rearing doves.[9]

The Messiah enters the palace. Herod's friends and relatives have gathered with the king this morning and are holding a judicial council.[10] The matter brought to their attention is extremely complex. The Messiah remembers the instructions given in his community's books of wisdom: "Do not speak until you have heard what they have to say . . . and when among princes, answer carefully."[11] He waits until a few of the friends and relatives have expressed their opinions and only then asks for permission to speak. He speaks softly and in his abundant wisdom unfolds the solution to the complex legal question.

At midday the king and his sons, friends, and relatives sit down in the great hall of the Caesareon for their midday meal. The decorations on the walls recall the wall paintings of Augustus's palace in Rome.[12] The first course consists of fish with a special sauce, a *garum* sauce sent from Rome to Herod's kitchens.[13] The main course is roasted doves from the king's dovecotes. For dessert, there are apples that have been sent to the king from Cumae in Italy.[14] During the meal Herod and the members of his court sip an Italian wine of the Philonianum variety. A large consignment of this wine from the vineyard of Lucio Laenio in southern Italy has recently arrived at the royal palace.[15] The

Messiah, who is scrupulous in his observance of dietary laws, is unable to touch the food served to the other guests. He receives a special portion of fruits and vegetables in a dish made of stone, which is resistant to impurities.[16]

After the meal, the famous writer and historian Nicholas of Damascus, who is permanently attached to Herod's court,[17] gets up. He reads aloud two letters that have just arrived from Rome. One is from Herod's sons Alexander and Aristobulus. The other is from the sons' host in Rome, the statesman and author Asinius Pollio.[18] Pollio has written about Augustus's return from his journey to the east. He has also related an event that has caused him great distress: the death of his friend, the celebrated poet Virgil.

Virgil had left Italy in 19 BCE to go to Athens. He had intended to remain in Greece for three years to complete the writing of his major work, the *Aeneid*. In Athens, however, Virgil met the Emperor Augustus, who was on his way back to Rome from the east, and Augustus persuaded the poet to return to Rome with him. On the way, Virgil fell sick. He never reached Rome, but died in Brindisium on 20 September in the year 19 BCE. Pollio added in his letter that before Virgil left Rome for Greece, he had appointed Varius his literary testator. Because he felt that the *Aeneid* was incomplete, he had ordered Varius to burn the work if he failed to return safely to Rome. However, Augustus commanded that the poet's instructions be ignored, and thus the great work was saved from the fire.[19]

When the reading of Pollio's letter is finished, the Messiah leaves the royal palace for the Essene Quarter. He enters one of the many ritual baths that exist in the quarter,[20] disrobes, and immerses himself in the bath. After this purification he puts on a white garment[21] given to him by one of the members of his community.

The members of the sect now gather for their evening meal. The atmosphere and menu here are completely different from those in Herod's palace. The participants sit at a long table headed by a priest and by the Messiah, who is the *nasi* (leader) of the community.[22] The baker walks along the length of the table, placing a piece of bread before each person. He is followed by the cook, who gives each member a dish of cooked vegetables.[23] First the priest blesses the bread and wine and eats a portion of the bread; then the Messiah blesses the bread and eats some of the piece placed in front of him. Only then may the others bless the bread and eat.[24] During the meal there is absolute silence.[25] At the end of the meal the members of the community make a final blessing and thank God for the food they have eaten.[26]

After the meal, the priest rises and blesses the Messiah as the *nasi* (leader) of the community:

> With your scepter may you devastate the land
> and by the breath of your lips may you kill the wicked
> > one . . .
>
> May he make your horns iron
> and your hooves bronze . . .
>
> for God raised you up as a rod for the rulers . . .
> and he shall strengthen you with his holy name.[27]

To the members of the Essene sect, the *nasi* is the Messiah, destined to rule over all the nations. The power would pass into his hands after a war in which the Messiah and his followers defeat the armies of the nations—first of all the army of Rome. The "wicked one" whom the Messiah would kill with the breath of his lips[28] is the "king of Kittim," which is a code name for the Roman Caesar Augustus.[29] This vision is not merely an abstraction. The Messiah and his followers are sitting with a scroll laid out in front of them. On the scroll is a detailed plan for the coming eschatological "war between the Sons of Light and the Sons of Darkness."

All these activities obviously take place in utmost secrecy. Were King Herod or one of his informers to hear of the aspirations of the Messiah and his followers, or the preparations for war against the Romans, he would undoubtedly sentence them to death. They would be taken to the Hyrcania fortress in the most desolate part of the Judean Desert, subjected to terrible tortures, and killed.[30] All members of the sect, however, have sworn a binding oath on joining the community to never reveal their secrets to strangers, even if tortured to death.[31] As a result, no one outside the sect knows about the messianic leader and the preparations for the war.

Late at night the Messiah goes to bed. Tomorrow he will again go to Herod's palace, sit in the company of the king's sons, and converse with Herod. The conversation will take place in the hall named after Emperor Augustus. No one taking part in the conversation would ever imagine that, only a few hours previously, their respectable guest had been sitting with the members of his community, planning the overthrow of Augustus and his army on the day of vengeance.[32]

This imaginary reconstruction of a day in the Messiah's life is based on literary sources from the period and on archaeological discoveries made in Qumran,[33] in Herod's palace at Massada, and in excavations in Jerusalem. It demonstrates the duality in

Figure 1.   The Scroll of the *War* between the Sons of Light and the Sons of Darkness.

the Messiah's life: on one hand, he was a respected guest at Herod's Roman-Hellenistic court; on the other, he and his followers longed for the time of holy war against the Romans. Yet this twofoldness was only part of the complexity of the figure of the Messiah. In order to learn more about him we now have to turn our eyes to the Dead Sea Scrolls.

THE MESSIANIC HYMNS

Early in 1947, a bedouin shepherd belonging to the Ta'mireh tribe of the Judean Desert was looking for a goat that had escaped from his flock. He stood at the entrance to a cave on a rocky slope overlooking the Dead Sea, near the site known as Hirbat Qumran, and tried his luck by throwing a stone into the cave. The stone struck an earthenware vessel, and the sound drew the shepherd inside. To his great surprise, he found a number of clay jars, one of which contained parchment scrolls. He sold the scrolls to a merchant of antiquities in Bethlehem.

E. L. Sukenik, professor of archaeology at the Hebrew University in Jerusalem, bought two of these scrolls from the Bethlehem merchant. Shortly afterwards, he managed to purchase another scroll. These along with other scrolls and scroll fragments found near Hirbat Qumran are known as the Dead Sea Scrolls.

Sukenik called one of the scrolls he had purchased "Thanksgivings Scroll" because it was made up of psalms most of which begin with the formula "I will give thanks unto the Lord." In these psalms the writer expresses gratitude to God for redeeming him from sin and bringing him close to His presence. The writer portrays himself as the head of a community of believers, and many scholars consequently believe that the scroll was written by

Figure 2. Cave 4, Qumran.

the "teacher of righteousness," the founder and original leader of the Qumran sect.

While the other scrolls found in the cave in Qumran were rolled up in a normal manner, the Thanksgivings Scroll was in an extraordinary condition—one that raises questions. It was stored in two separate parts. The part opened first contained three sheets of parchment. These sheets were not rolled inside one another; rather, each one was folded separately. Upon examination, it became clear that the sheets had not been separated by the bedouin when he took the scrolls out of the jars, but that the different parts of the Thanksgivings Scroll had been stored that way in antiquity. The second part of the scroll was a squeezed and crumpled mass consisting of about seventy large and small scroll fragments.[34]

Apparently, before it was stored the scroll had been deliberately disfigured. One of the members of the sect had torn apart the sheets of the scroll, folded up three of these sheets, and torn up the others into a multitude of fragments and compressed them into a single mass. There was clear intention to disfigure the scroll. Yet the scroll was not totally destroyed. Someone from the sect—whether the same person who had disfigured it or someone else—had stored the torn sheets and crumpled fragments in the cave where the sacred writings of the sect were put. How are we to understand this mixture of destruction and preservation?

It seems that this particular copy of the Thanksgivings Scroll aroused mixed feelings among the members of the sect. One can understand the desire to preserve this scroll, which after all was one of the sacred writings of the sect, but what created the urge to tear it up and destroy it? Was there something in this particu-

Figure 3.   The torn sheets of the Thanksgivings Scroll.

lar scroll that members of the sect regarded as heretical matter needing to be suppressed?

Two unusual hymns, which I believe could indeed have aroused a great deal of opposition among some of the members of the sect, had been included in this scroll. Only a few remnants of

these hymns have been preserved among the crumpled fragments found in what is now known as cave 1 in Qumran; but, as
luck would have it, three other manuscripts found later in cave 4
contain versions of these hymns, and with their help we are able
to reconstruct the text of the fragments from cave 1.[35]

These hymns are different from the other thanksgiving psalms
both in their language and in their forms of benediction.[36] The
atmosphere prevailing in these hymns is also essentially different from the general atmosphere of the psalms. The thanksgiving psalms are imbued with a heavy sense of guilt. Their assumption is that humans be liberated from their guilty, sinful
condition only through the grace of God.[37] In these hymns,
on the other hand, this sense of guilt is completely absent;
we learn, on the contrary, that sin and guilt have disappeared
as though they had never been.[38] For all these reasons, scholars have reached the conclusion that these hymns were not part
of the original Thanksgivings collection, but were inserted at a
later date.[39]

The first hymn is written in the first person. Based on the different manuscripts, we can reconstruct the hymn as follows:[40]

[Who] has been despised like [me? And who]
has been rejected [of men] like me? [And who] compares to
　m[e in enduring] evil?
. . . .
Who is like me among the angels?
[I] am the beloved of the king, a companion of the ho[ly ones].

The figure represented in this hymn is complex and fascinat-
ing. We see a very marked dichotomy in the self-image of the
writer. He sees himself as possessing divine attributes, but at the

Figure 4.   The first messianic hymn—version 1: 4QHe frg. 1–2.

same time he views himself in the image of the "suffering servant" in Isaiah 53. Of the "suffering servant" it is written: "He was despised and rejected of men; a man of sorrows, and acquainted with grief" (Isaiah 53:3). The writer of the hymn says:

> And who] has been despised like [me? And who]
> has been rejected [of men] like me?

Again, we read of the "suffering servant": "Surely he has borne our griefs and carried our sorrows" (Isaiah 53:4). Likewise, the writer of the hymn says of himself:

> [And who] compares to m[e in enduring] evil?

The hymn's author reaches the height of audacity when he says:

> Who is like me among the angels (*elim*)?

The temerity of this expression becomes all the more evident when we realize that it is based on a verse in the Bible that refers to God: "Who is like thee, O Lord, among the gods (*elim*)?" (Exodus 15:11). The author of the hymn takes the praise given to God in the Bible and uses it to glorify himself! The term *elim* used by the author refers here to the angels.[41] The writer is boasting that none of the angels in heaven can compare to him. Such audacious use of a biblical verse could surely have led to the disfiguration of the copy of the Thanksgivings Scroll later.

The writer also calls himself the "beloved," or "friend," of the king. This expression usually refers to a king of flesh and blood,[42] but in the immediate context of this hymn the king in question is God. This is confirmed by the end of the sentence, where the writer describes himself as "a companion of the holy ones," that is, a friend of the angels.[43]

This hymn, known among scholars as the Self-Glorification Hymn, exists in another version, which also bears the imprint of this complex and many-sided personality. At the beginning of the second version, we learn that the writer experienced sitting on a splendid throne in heaven in a council of gods/angels:[44]

> a throne of power in the angelic council. No king of yore
>   will sit therein.
> I sit [. . .] in heaven.

The writer adds that he is regarded as belonging with the angels and dwells in their council:

> I shall be reckoned with the angels, my dwelling is in the
>   holy council.

He claims to have attained a superhuman condition, evidenced in the elimination of fleshly desires and the capacity to bear physical suffering:

[My] desi[re] is not of the flesh,

. . . .

Who has born[e all] afflictions like me? Who compares to
me [in enduri]ng evil?

As in the first version of the hymn, we see here a strong dichotomy in the character of the speaker; he claims to be simultaneously the most despised and the most honored of men:

[W]ho has been accounted despicable like me, yet who is like
me in my glory?

The writer also boasts of his incomparable talents as a teacher
and judge:

Who can associate with me and thus compare with my
judgment?

And just above:

no teaching compares
[to my teaching].[45]

When he opens his mouth, no one interrupts him, and no one
who hears him can grasp all he says:

Who could cut off m[y words]? And who could measure the
flow of my speech? [46]

Who is speaking in the hymns? Are these the actual words of
an extraordinary personality, or have they been placed in the
mouth of an imaginary figure?

Some scholars have thought these words were meant to be
those of the imaginary figure of the priest-Messiah, or teacher, at
the "end of days," [47] but it is hard to accept this idea. Although

Figure 5.   The first messianic hymn—version 2: 4Q491 frg. 11, col. 1.

there are descriptions of future messianic figures in the Dead Sea
literature, there is nothing remotely like this hymn written in the
first person. Similarly, there is nothing resembling the audacity
and self-aggrandizement reflected in this hymn. As J. J. Collins,
a leading scholar of this literature, says:

> [N]owhere else in the corpus of the scrolls do we find words
> placed in the mouth of either Messiah, and so there is no
> parallel for a speech such as we find in 4Q491 by a messianic
> figure. Neither is there any parallel for such claims by any-
> one else.[48]

Further, the combination of divine status and suffering in this
hymn is unknown in Jewish literature. Hence, it is hard to believe
that someone would create such an unusual imaginary messianic
figure. The unique character of the hymn causes us to think that
it is the original expression of a historical personality active in

the Qumran community. In my opinion, there is evidence that the speaker in the hymn was a leader of the Qumran sect who saw himself as the Messiah and was so regarded by his community.[49]

The first hymn, the Self-Glorification Hymn, is followed in all four of its manuscripts by a second hymn[50] that calls on the community to thank God for his mercies. The scholars who have pondered the identity of the speaker in the first hymn have considered the question without reference to the second hymn, but the fact that in all manuscripts the two hymns appear in succession shows that there must be a close connection between them. Moreover, in the second hymn, as in the first, there are clear indications in both language and content that it did not originally belong to the Thanksgivings Scroll.[51] Further, these are the only psalms in the Thanksgivings Scroll that were found in two different versions. For all of these reasons, in my opinion, the hymns ought to be seen as two parts of a single composition. I believe that one cannot consider the identity of the speaker in the first hymn without considering the content of the second.

The connection between the first and second hymns is evident in the content of the two hymns. The speaker in the first hymn describes his experience of sitting in heaven in the company of the gods/angels in the first person:

> I sit [. . .] in heaven,
> I shall be reckoned with the angels.

In the second hymn we find a description of this same experience expressed in the third person:

> Great is God who ac[ts wonderfully],
> for he casts down the haughty spirit . . . and lifts up the poor
> from the dust to [the eternal height],

and to the clouds he magnifies him in stature, and [he is] with
the heavenly beings in the assembly of the community.[52]

This description provides us with valuable information about
the speaker in the first hymn, who in his own words had sat in
heaven surrounded by angels. Here he is described as a wretch
who had groveled in the dust, but whom God had raised "to the
clouds."

The second hymn is essentially a call to the members of the
community to thank God for the salvation he has bestowed on
them. The speaker begins:

Sing praise, O beloved ones, sing to the king of
[glory, rejoice in the congre]gation of God, ring out joy in
the tents of salvation.

Later in the hymn, one finds a description of a dramatic change
that has taken place in the fortunes of the sect:

[. . . and wickedness perishes . . .]
.   .   .   .
deceit [end]s, and there are no witless perversities; light
appears,
grief [disappears], and groaning flees; peace appears, terror
ceases; a fountain is opened for [eternal] bles[sing]
and [for] healing for all times . . . iniquity ends.

The age depicted here is a time of redemption in which
wickedness, sin, and mourning have disappeared and been replaced by the light of salvation. Redemption is not described here
as a prophetic vision for the future or as an object of prayer, as it
is in other places in the Thanksgivings Scroll,[53] but as an already
existing reality.

Figure 6.   The second messianic hymn—version 1: 4QHa frg. 7, col. 1 and 2.

The people of Qumran expected the coming of a Messiah who would bring them atonement for their sins. In one of the Qumranic scrolls, the Damascus Covenant, we read that the laws it contains would be valid until the advent of the Messiah. The Messiah would bring the members of the sect an atonement superior to that which could be obtained through meal or sin-offerings:

> And this is the explication of the rules by which they shall be [go]verned until the rise of the anointed of Aaron and Israel,

and he will atone their iniquity better than through [me]al and sin-offerings.[54]

While the Damascus Covenant describes the messianic atonement as a hope for the future, in our hymn atonement and forgiveness of sins have already taken place.

The era of messianic redemption is depicted here as a contemporary reality. Indeed, in version two of the second hymn, the members of the sect are called upon to rejoice before God and to praise him for establishing "the horn of [his] Mess[iah]":[55]

[. . . Rejoice,] you righteous among the angels [. . .] in the holy dwelling, hymn [him]
[. . . pro]claim the sound of a ringing cry [. . .] in eternal joy, without [. . .]
[. . .] to establish the horn of [his] Mess[iah][56]
[. . .] to make known his power in might [. . .]

Who was this Messiah whose "horn" was "established" by God?

We would not be mistaken if we identified the Messiah referred to here with the speaker in the first hymn—the Self-Glorification Hymn. This man's description of himself as sitting in heaven on a divine throne corresponds to the biblical descriptions of the figure of the Messiah.[57] The point of view one finds in the second hymn—that redemption and forgiveness have already come—is apparently connected with the appearance of this personality.

As we have seen, the speaker in the first hymn describes himself in terms reminiscent of the "suffering servant":

And who] has been despised like [me? And who]
has been rejected [of men] like me?

Who has born[e all] afflictions like me? Who compares to
m[e in enduri]ng evil? [58]

The description in the second hymn of the hero being mag-
nified "to the clouds" also corresponds to the description of the
"servant of God" or "suffering servant" in Isaiah: "Behold, my
servant shall prosper, he shall be exalted and lifted up, and shall
be very high" (Isaiah 52:13).

The "suffering servant" in Isaiah bore the sins of his community and atoned for them:

Surely he hath borne our griefs and carried our sorrows . . .
But he was wounded for our transgressions, he was bruised
    for our iniquities . . .
yet he bore the sin of many, and made intercession for the
    transgressors. (Isaiah 53:4, 5, 12)

In view of the close connection we find in the Dead Sea literature between the coming of the Messiah and the forgiveness
of sins,[59] one may suppose that the speaker in the first hymn,
who saw himself in terms of the "suffering servant" described by
Isaiah, was regarded by his community as someone who through
his sufferings had atoned for the sins of all the members of his sect.

JESUS AND THE HERO OF THE HYMNS

Jesus was born about the time that King Herod died (4 BCE) and
was crucified in Jerusalem about 30 CE. Who was the historical
Jesus?[60] How did Jesus see himself? The dominant approach in
New Testament studies declares that Jesus did not consider himself the Messiah.[61] According to this school, Jesus did not iden-

tify himself with the messianic figures of the "son of man" of the Book of Daniel[62] and the "suffering servant" of Isaiah 53. Rather, this identification was made by his disciples after his death. R. Bultmann, the chief representative of this school, commented:

> Of course, the attempt is made to carry the idea of the suffering Son of Man into Jesus' own outlook by assuming that Jesus regarded himself as Deutero-Isaiah's Servant of God who suffers and dies for the sinner, and fused together the two ideas Son of Man and Servant of God into the single figure of the suffering, dying and rising Son of Man. At the very outset, the misgivings which must be raised as to the historicity of the predictions of the passion speak against this attempt. In addition, the tradition of Jesus' sayings reveals no trace of consciousness on his part of being the Servant of God of Isaiah 53. The messianic interpretation of Isaiah 53 was discovered in the Christian Church and even in it not immediately.[63]

I think the messianic hymns from Qumran cast doubt on Bultmann's conclusions. The hero of the hymns claims divine status. He claims to be superior to the angels[64] and describes himself as taking a seat in heaven surrounded by the angels,[65] thus clearly comparing himself to the biblical God.[66] Simultaneously, he depicts himself as "despised and rejected of men" and claims

> Who has born[e all] afflictions like me? Who compares to
>   me [in enduri]ng evil?[67]

He thus identifies himself with the "suffering servant" in Isaiah. This combination of divine status and suffering is unknown in the history of the messianic idea prior to these hymns.

Thus, the messianic interpretation of Isaiah 53 was *not* discovered in the Christian Church. It was already developed by the Messiah of Qumran. In view of these facts, we should consider the possibility that the depiction of Jesus as a combination of the "son of man" and the "suffering servant" was not a later invention of the Church. Perhaps the historical Jesus really did see himself in this way, since a fusion of this kind had already been made by his predecessor, the Messiah from Qumran.

What was the nature of the historical connection between Jesus and the Qumran Messiah? Is it possible that Jesus knew him personally? From the hymns themselves it is difficult to obtain clear historical evidence indicating the period of activity of the messianic leader. The four manuscripts that have come down to us containing the messianic hymns with their two versions may all be dated by their script to a period between 50 BCE and the beginning of the Christian era,[68] which was the time of Herod's rule.[69] This information enables us to ascertain that the messianic movement existed in the second half of the first century BCE, at the latest. However, the time when the copies of the hymns we possess were written is not necessarily the time when the hymns themselves were composed. We can not rule out the possibility that they were composed earlier and that earlier copies were lost and have not come down to us.

We must find an Archimedean point outside the hymns that can provide us with information about the existence of a messianic leader in the Qumran sect in the period we have mentioned. Such a point is to be found, in my opinion, in the group of apocalyptic writings we shall discuss in the next chapter.

CHAPTER TWO

After Three Days

We will start our search for the historical setting of the Qumranic Messiah with a discussion of two apocalyptic works. In my view, these apocalypses tell us about the violent death of the Messiah of Qumran. Our first task will be to date the events described in these works. In an apocalyptic work the author usually describes the events of his time as a prophecy of the future. This is why apocalyptic works should be interpreted against the background of the historical events of the time they were composed. As I argue in detail, the content of these works can be clearly understood in light of the political situation in the Roman Empire during the second half of the first century BCE, just prior to Jesus' life and ministry.

In the year 44 BCE Julius Caesar was murdered by a group of conspirators headed by Brutus and Cassius. After the murder, Caesar's will was examined. In his will Caesar had declared that he had adopted Octavian, the son of his niece Attia, as his son. This adopted son was now given the name of the murdered

Figures 7–8.   Portrait of Octavian as Caesar Divi
filius opposite that of the Divus Iulius (Sestercius
of Octavian, ca. 40 BCE).

Caesar, and he became Caesar Octavianus. Octavian—later to
be given the title "Augustus"—was at that time a youth of nine-
teen. He had to struggle for power in Rome against rivals who
were older and more experienced—especially Mark Anthony.

Octavian's main effort at that time was directed toward gain-
ing divine honors for the murdered Caesar; for if his adoptive
father was recognized as divine, Octavian would as a matter of
course also be given divine status. Wishing to stress that he was
the son of the "divine Julius," Octavian called himself *divi filius*,
which means "son of God" or "son of the deified." This title appeared on his coins.[1]

In the years following Caesar's murder, cruel wars took place.
At first, Octavian and Mark Anthony fought together against
Caesar's murderers and their supporters. Once they had overcome their enemies, they divided the empire between them. Octavius was based in Rome and ruled the western countries, while
Mark Anthony established himself in Alexandria and ruled the
eastern provinces.[2] Mark Anthony's close relations with Cleopatra, queen of Egypt, caused great friction between himself and

Octavius, resulting eventually in the sea battle at Actium in 31 BCE. The fortune of the battle was still undecided when

> on a sudden Cleopatra's sixty ships were seen hoisting sail and making out to sea in full flight, right through the ships that were engaged. . . . Here it was that Anthony showed to all the world that he was no longer actuated by the thoughts and motives of a commander . . . or indeed by his own judgment at all. . . . For, as if he had been part of her (i.e., Cleopatra) and must move with her wheresoever she went, as soon as he saw her ship sailing away, he abandoned all that were fighting and spending their life for him, and . . . followed her.[3]

Thus were Anthony and Cleopatra defeated by Octavian's fleet. They fled to Alexandria, where they committed suicide.

I believe that these dramatic events are reflected in the apocalypse known as the Oracle of Hystaspes.

THE ORACLE OF HYSTASPES

The prophecy of Hystaspes was first mentioned in the middle of the second century CE in the writings of Justin Martyr, who was killed by the Roman authorities for his Christian beliefs. He related that the Roman rulers decreed a death sentence on anyone who read this prophesy, which foretold the fall of the Roman Empire. He added that despite this wicked decree, he and his friends continued to read the prophecy.[4] The Church Father Clement of Alexandria related that Paul of Tarsus had both recommended reading the prophecy of Hystaspes and quoted from it.[5]

The mythical Hystaspes, to whom the Oracle was ascribed,

was a king of Media who was supposed to have lived before the Trojan War. But the Persian identity disguises the fact that the apocalyptic work was written by a Jew about the Jewish people and Jerusalem.[6] Passages from the Oracle of Hystaspes are preserved in a book by the Church Father Lactantius (ca. 300 CE), who was known as the Christian Cicero.

In his prophesy Hystaspes spoke of two kings. Regarding the first, who would rule over Asia, Hystaspes said:

> He shall harass the world with his intolerable rule . . . and
> shall meditate new designs in his breast, that he may establish
> the government for himself. . . . And finally, he shall change
> the name of the empire and transfer its seat.[7]

After that, another king would come,[8] more terrible than the first, and would destroy him. Hystaspes described this second king: "[H]e will constitute and call himself God and will order himself to be worshipped as the son of God."[9]

Who were these two kings?

Hystaspes said that the first king, who ruled over Asia, would change the name of the empire and transfer its capital. These statements correspond exactly to the accusations that the supporters of Octavian-Augustus made against Mark Anthony on account of his relations with Cleopatra.

In 40 BCE, Anthony married Octavian-Augustus's sister Octavia, following an agreement between the two rivals reached at Brindisium in that year. The agreement and the marriage aroused great hopes among the Romans, who were tired of the endless wars, but these hopes were dashed when Anthony returned to his lover, Cleopatra, and married her. The rivalry between Anthony and Octavian-Augustus reached its culmination in the year 32 BCE, when Anthony divorced Octavia and expelled her from his home. In response, Octavian-Augustus unlawfully took Anthony's will out of the keeping of the vestal priestesses in Rome and read it before the Senate. In the will Anthony had written that even if he died in Rome, he wished to be brought to Alexandria and buried next to Cleopatra. The will was taken as evidence for claims that Anthony wished to transfer the capital of the empire to Alexandria. The Senate ordered a war against the Egyptian queen, and this led to the battle of Actium between Augustus's fleet and that of Anthony and Cleopatra.[10] The Roman historian Dio Cassius related[11] that it was believed in Rome that "if Anthony should prevail, he would bestow their city to Cleopatra and transfer the seat of power to Egypt."[12]

In Hystaspes' vision it is said that the first king "shall meditate new designs in his breast, that he may establish the government for himself. . . . And finally, he shall change the name of the empire and transfer its seat." This king can thus be identified as Mark Anthony. According to Hystaspes, the first king would be destroyed by the second king. This king was Augustus, who prevailed over Anthony. Hystaspes said about the second king: "He will . . . call himself God and will order himself to be worshipped as the son of God"; indeed, Octavian-Augustus called himself *divi filius*—"son of God."

According to Hystaspes the second king, the "son of God," would be a false prophet who would bring fire down from heaven:

> [H]e will also be a prophet of lies, and he will constitute and
> call himself God and will order himself to be worshipped
> as the son of God, and power will be given to him to do

signs and wonders by the sight of which he may entice men to adore him. He will command fire to come down from heaven.[13]

Why was Augustus, the "son of God," described as a false prophet?

THE FALSE PROPHET
IN THE BOOK OF REVELATION

The figure of a false prophet who brings fire down from heaven is also familiar to us from the famous vision in chapter 13 of the Book of Revelation in the New Testament.[14] Two beasts are described in this vision.

The first beast, with seven heads and ten horns, rose out of the sea. One of the heads of this beast was gravely wounded, but the wound was healed. All the inhabitants of the earth worshipped this beast. Later a second beast rose: "And I beheld another beast coming up out of the earth; and he had two horns like a lamb, and he spoke as a dragon" (Revelation 13:11). By means of signs and wonders, including making fire come down from heaven, this beast persuaded the inhabitants of the earth to make an image of the first beast and worship it. "And he doeth great wonders, so that he maketh fire come down from heaven on the earth in the sight of men" (13:13).

The second beast closely resembles the figure of the false prophet, the "son of God," in Hystaspes.

Throughout the history of Christianity, all kinds of interpretations have been suggested for the vision of the two beasts, but it seems that until now no really convincing explanation has been given. In my opinion, the key to understanding the vision is to realize that John, who appears to have written the Book of Revelation around 80 CE,[15] made use here of an older composition written at the beginning of the first century, during the reign of Augustus.

The second beast is described as having two horns like a lamb's horns and speaking like a dragon. This strange combination of a dragon and a lamb's horns[16] can be adequately explained by the propaganda concerning Augustus's divine origin. The figure of a kid or a goat with two horns—the Capricorn—had an important place in the myth of the divinity of Augustus. The Capricorn was the sign of the month of Augustus's conception. The importance Augustus gave to the sign of the Capricorn is ascribed by Suetonius to what the astrologer Theogenes told Augustus in his youth:

> [A]t Apollonia, Augustus mounted with Agrippa to the studio of the astrologer Theogenes. Agrippa was the first to try his fortune, and when a great and almost incredible career was predicted to him, Augustus persisted in concealing the time of his birth and in refusing to disclose it, through diffidence and fear that he might be found to be less eminent. When at last he gave it unwillingly and hesitatingly, and only after many urgent requests, Theogenes sprang up and threw himself at his feet. From that time on Augustus had such faith in his destiny that he made his horoscope public, and issued a silver coin stamped with the sign of the constellation Capricorn, under which he was born.[17]

The Capricorn does indeed appear on various coins minted by Augustus. A coin minted in Spain shows a goat with two horns

Figure 9.   Capricorn with the
inscription "Augustus" (denarius,
minted in Spain ca. 17–15 BCE).

that support a globe, and underneath is the inscription "Augustus." Augustus also placed the sign of the Capricorn on some of the standards of the Roman legions. As classicist J. R. Fears explained,[18] the Capricorn signified that Augustus reigned with the favor of the gods and had been chosen by them to rule the world.

The beast with two lamb's horns is described as speaking like a dragon. The dragon symbolized Augustus's connection with the god Apollo.[19] Dio Cassius claimed that Julius Caesar chose Octavian-Augustus as his successor because he was influenced by the story told by Attia, mother of Augustus and niece of Julius, that she had conceived him from the god Apollo:

> He was influenced largely by Attia's emphatic declaration
> that the youth had been engendered by Apollo, for while
> sleeping once in his temple, she said, she thought she had
> an intercourse with a dragon and it was this that caused her
> at the end of the allotted time to bear a son.[20]

Suetonius, who also related this story in *The Lives of the Caesars*,[21] added that after the incident in the temple, a dragon-shaped spot appeared on Attia's body. The dragon symbolized Apollo's title, "Pythic Apollo," which he gained when he slew Python, the terrible dragon that lived in the cave at Delphi.[22]

The legend of the miraculous birth of Augustus first appeared in an epigram written by Domitius Marsus, a poet who was one of the ruler's friends.[23] Augustus became still more closely connected with the god after his victory at Actium, which took place near the temple of Apollo. The contemporary poet Propertius described the god Apollo standing on Augustus's vessel and shooting arrows at Cleopatra's ships.[24] After this victory Augustus built a splendid temple to Apollo near his home on the Palatine Hill.[25] On a colonnade near this temple a statue of Apollo was erected bearing the likeness of Augustus,[26] and on coins minted in Asia Minor after the battle of Actium, Augustus was represented as Apollo.[27]

The beast with the two lamb's horns who spoke like a dragon was Augustus, who represented himself as Apollo. The god Apollo was known for his gifts of prophecy, the most notable expression of which was the oracle at Delphi. Powers of prophecy were likewise ascribed to Augustus.[28] The author of the vision in the Book of Revelation was arguing against Augustus's propaganda, maintaining that Augustus was not a true prophet, but a false prophet who spoke like a dragon. The prophesying dragon was Python,[29] the monstrous serpent of Delphi that was slain by Apollo. While Augustus used the myth of Apollo in order to impart the god's divinity to himself, the author of the vision used the same myth in order to represent Augustus as a monstrous dragon.[30]

In the vision of the two beasts, the false prophet persuaded all the inhabitants of the earth to worship the image of the first

Figure 10.   The Apollonian snake winds around the tripod (glass cameo).

beast (Revelation 13:12). As R. H. Charles explains at length,[31] the first beast was the Roman Empire. One of its heads received a deadly wound, but the beast recovered. That blow to the head was delivered by the conspirators who murdered Julius Caesar,[32] but the Roman Empire recovered and continued to dominate the world. Hence, the image of the first beast, which the false prophet had persuaded all the inhabitants of the earth to worship, was the statue representing the Roman Empire. This is explained by Suetonius,[33] who reported that Augustus ordered the placement of a statue of the goddess Roma, symbol of the Roman Empire, next to the statue of the emperor in the temples erected in his honor. Augustus was the false prophet of the imperial cult to the statue of Roma.

In the vision of the two beasts in chapter 13 of Revelation and in the Oracle of Hystaspes one finds a polemic against the propaganda that represented Augustus as a ruler with divine attributes[34] and against the imperial cult that existed in his time.[35] Hystaspes criticized Augustus and accused him of creating a cult in which he was worshipped as God and as the "son of God," and the Book of Revelation attacked the second element of the imperial cult—the worship of the goddess Roma, symbol of the empire.

THE SLAYING OF THE MESSIAHS
AND THEIR SUBSEQUENT RESURRECTION

The Oracle of Hystaspes described the coming of a great prophet:

> When the time draws nigh, a great prophet shall be sent
> from God to turn men to the knowledge of God. And he will
> receive the power of doing wonderful things. Whenever men
> shall not hear him, he will shut up the heaven, and cause it
> to withhold its rains; he will turn water into blood . . . and
> if anyone shall endeavor to injure him, fire shall come forth
> out of his mouth and shall burn that man. By these prodigies
> and powers he shall turn many to the worship of God.[36]

The second king, the "son of God," described as a false prophet, will wage war on the prophet of God and slay him:

> He shall fight against the prophet of God and shall overcome and slay him, and shall suffer him to lie unburied; but after the third day he shall come to life again; and while all look on and wonder, he shall be caught up to heaven.[37]

The false prophet, the "son of God," is Augustus. Hystaspes thus claims that Augustus, the false prophet, fought the true prophet sent from God and killed him. Augustus then prevented the corpse of the true prophet from being buried, but after three days this prophet rose again and ascended to heaven.

A parallel tradition is found in the story of the two witnesses in chapter 11 of the Book of Revelation. The same miracles that Hystaspes attributes to the prophet of God are ascribed to the two witnesses.[38] The final destiny of the witnesses resembles that of the prophet:

> And when they have finished their testimony, the beast that ascends from the abyss will make war upon them and conquer them and kill them.
> And their dead bodies will lie in the street of the great city which is allegorically called Sodom and Egypt, where also our Lord was crucified.
> For three days and a half, men from the peoples and tribes and tongues and nations will gaze at their dead bodies and refuse to let them be placed in a tomb.
> But after three and a half days a breath of life from God entered them, and they stood on their feet, and great fear fell on those who saw them.

And they heard a loud voice from heaven saying to them,
"Come up hither!" And in the sight of their foes they went
up to heaven in a cloud. (Revelation 11:7–9, 11–12)

In their essentials the two accounts are alike. The main difference is that Hystaspes speaks of a single prophet, while the Book
of Revelation speaks about two prophesying witnesses.[39] The two
witnesses are described as two olive trees standing before the Lord
of the whole earth (11:4). This is unmistakable use of the termi-
nology of Zechariah 4:11, 14: "Then I said to him, 'What are
these two olive-trees . . . ?' Then he said, 'These are the two
anointed who stand by the Lord of the whole earth.'" "Two
olive-trees" and "two anointed" indicate two Messiahs who are
anointed with oil. The prophet Zechariah was hinting here at
the two leaders of his period, which was the time of the return to
Zion: the royal Messiah Zerubbabel, son of Shealtiel, and the
priestly Messiah Jeshua, son of Jozadak. This being the case, it
would seem that the two witnesses in the Book of Revelation are
two messianic leaders: a royal Messiah and a priestly Messiah.[40]

Hystaspes says that the prophet of God was killed by the "son
of God," whom we have identified as Augustus. In the Book of
Revelation, the two witnesses/Messiahs[41] were killed by a beast
that ascends from an abyss (*abyssos*) (Revelation 11:7), which is
also a designation for Augustus and his army.[42]

According to the Book of Revelation, the two witnesses/
Messiahs were killed in a battle in the streets of Jerusalem.[43]
When did this battle take place?

In the first two verses of chapter 11 of the Book of Revelation,
before the story of the two witnesses, we read:

> I was given a measuring rod like a staff, and I was told: "Rise
> and measure the temple of God and the altar and those
> that worship there.
> But do not measure the court outside the temple; leave that
> out, for it is given over to the nations.

We learn from this that in the battle in which the two witnesses
were killed the Roman soldiers penetrated the courtyard of the
Temple, but the Temple itself and the altar remained untouched.
This gives us the key to the precise time of the event.

King Herod, who ruled the land of Israel by favor of the Romans, died in 4 BCE, and after his death a great revolt broke out
in the country.[44] The revolt was directed against Herod's successor, Archelaus, and the Roman army, which supported him. During the revolt Roman soldiers entered the courtyard of the
Temple and plundered its treasury. The soldiers set fire to the
outer chambers in the courtyard,[45] but did not enter the Temple
itself or the inner precincts where the altar was situated. This
corresponds exactly to the opening verses of chapter 11 of the
Book of Revelation, which say that the courtyard of the Temple,
but not the Temple or the altar, was trampled by the nations.[46]

The revolt of 4 BCE was brutally crushed by Quintilius Varus,
Augustus's governor in Syria.[47] Varus arrived from Syria[48] with
two legions and some other forces. The soldiers of his army sowed
destruction in their wake and abused women;[49] Varus crucified
two thousand of the rebels, and others were taken prisoner and
sold into slavery.[50] The Jews placed the responsibility for the bru-
tal suppression of the revolt and the burning of the courtyard of
the Temple on the Roman Caesar Augustus. This charge is ex-

pressed in two verses in the pseudepigraphical work *The Assumption of Moses*, which describes the suppression:

> Into their *parts cohorts* and a powerful king of the west shall
> come, *who* shall conquer them: and he shall take them captive,
> and burn a part of their temple with fire, (and) shall crucify
> some around their colony.[51]

The powerful king who came from the west was Augustus, who is represented here as a cruel executioner.[52] In the eyes of the Jews he was responsible for the actions of his governor and his soldiers. In light of this background we can understand why Augustus is depicted so hatefully in the sources we have examined.

The Oracle of Hystaspes speaks of the killing of the "prophet of God" and the Book of Revelation relates the killing of two Messiahs. How is one to explain the difference between the two sources? It seems that one of the two messianic leaders was more prominent than the other. Hystaspes referred only to the prominent one, who is described as the "prophet of God" in order to create an opposition to the "prophet of lies"—Augustus.

In both the sources we find motifs familiar to us from the Dead Sea literature. Hystaspes described the rout of the false prophet and his army by the sword of God, which descends from heaven. This description parallels the description of Herev-El (the sword of God) in the Scroll of the War between the Sons of Light and the Sons of Darkness.[53] In the Book of Revelation we find the story of the two messianic witnesses. In the Dead Sea literature we find two Messiahs—a priestly Messiah and a royal Messiah.[54]

We can assume that the tradition concerning the killing of the prophet or the Messiahs that we find in these works came from the members of the Qumran sect or some circle close to them. It thus appears that the messianic leaders whose deaths were related in these sources belonged to the Qumran community.

As the two messianic leaders were killed in 4 BCE, they surely were active in the period previous to that year—that is, during the reign of King Herod (37–4 BCE). As we have seen, all four copies of the messianic hymns were written precisely at that period. One can therefore assume that one of the two Messiahs killed in 4 BCE was the hero of the messianic hymns from Qumran.

Was the protagonist of these hymns the royal Messiah or the priestly Messiah? The hero of the hymns did not have any priestly attributes; on the other hand, he spoke of sitting on a "throne of power" and mentioned a crown.[55] From this we may deduce he was the royal Messiah. There was also the other "olive tree," a priestly messiah.

LOOKING AT THE PIERCED MESSIAH

The messianic hymns suggest that for a few years the members of the Qumran sect thought that the era of redemption had arrived. They believed that a new age had begun in which mourning had vanished and light and joy prevailed. But the reality proved to be different. Their messianic leader was slain by the Roman soldiers and his body was left in the street unburied for three days, like that of a criminal.[56]

We have no historical sources that describe the feelings of the members of the Qumran sect on seeing the pierced body of the Messiah lying in the street. However, a historical analogy can help us here. We can turn to Gershom Scholem's observations on the crisis that overtook the disciples of Shabbetai Zevi, a seventeenth-century Jewish messianic leader, after he left Judaism and became a Muslim. The feelings of the followers of the Qumran Messiah previous to the year 4 BCE no doubt resembled those of Shabbetai Zevi's followers before the crisis caused by his change of religion:

> They were to believe in perfect simplicity that a new era
> of history was being ushered in and that they themselves had
> already begun to inhabit a new and redeemed world. Such
> a belief could not but have a profound effect on those who
> held it: their innermost feelings, which assured them of the
> presence of messianic reality, seemed entirely in harmony
> with the outward course of events.

Crisis erupted for the members of the Qumran sect when the events of the year 4 BCE proved to be in total contradiction to their feelings about the coming of redemption. A similar situation is described by Gershom Scholem:

> [F]or the first time, a contradiction appeared between the
> two levels of the drama of redemption, that of the subjective
> experience on the one hand and that of the objective histori-
> cal facts on the other. . . . Above all, the "believers," those
> who remained loyal to the inward experience, were com-
> pelled to find an answer to the simple question: what could
> be the value of a historical reality that had proved to be so
> bitterly disappointing, and, how might it be related to the
> hopes it had betrayed?[57]

The answer to this question can be found above all in the sources that describe the death of the Messiah: the Oracle of Hystaspes and chapter 11 of the Book of Revelation.

We can infer from these sources that the believers found a major key to understanding the catastrophe in the Book of Daniel. They interpreted the vision of the fourth beast in the seventh chapter of the Book of Daniel as a prophecy about Augustus and the Roman Empire: the Roman Empire under Augustus was that beast, which devoured and trampled the whole earth.[58]

Daniel states that the fourth beast "made war with the saints, and prevailed over them" (7:21).[59] The believers interpreted this verse as a prediction of the military confrontation between the Messiah and his followers and the soldiers of Augustus.[60] According to this interpretation, the defeat of the "saints" (the Messiah and his followers) by the Roman army had been foretold in the Scriptures.[61]

Another Scripture that served as a basis for understanding the Messiah's tragic fate was a verse in Zechariah (12:10): "They shall look on him whom they have pierced."[62] This verse was interpreted as referring to the Messiah, whose pierced body was left in the street for three days for all to see.[63]

We saw in chapter 1 how the Qumran Messiah appropriated for himself the description of the "suffering servant" in Isaiah 53:3–4:

> He was despised and rejected by men; a man of sorrows, and
>   acquainted with grief; and as one from whom men hide
>   their faces he was despised, and we esteemed him not.
> Surely he has borne our griefs and carried our sorrows; yet
>   we esteemed him stricken, smitten by God, and afflicted.

These verses undoubtedly gained a completely new significance after the death of the Messiah. The fact that the body of the Messiah had been left unburied in the street like that of a criminal could now be explained by the following passage from the same chapter in Isaiah:

> And they made his grave with the wicked, and with a rich man in his death, although he had done no violence, and there was no deceit in his mouth.
>
> Therefore I will divide him a portion with the great, and he shall divide the spoil with the strong; because he poured out his soul to death, and was numbered with the transgressors; yet he bore the sin of many, and made intercession for the transgressors. (Isaiah 53:9, 12)

Thus after the Messiah's death his believers created a "catastrophic" ideology.[64] The rejection of the Messiah, his humiliation, and his death were thought to have been foretold in the Scriptures and to be necessary stages in the process of redemption. The disciples believed that the humiliated and pierced Messiah had been resurrected after three days and that he was due to reappear on earth as redeemer, victor, and judge.

Daniel prophesied that the fourth beast would be destroyed and the kingdom would be given to the "son of man," whom Daniel described as sitting on a heavenly throne and as coming in the clouds of heaven.[65]

The disciples and followers of the Qumranic Messiah believed that he had been resurrected after three days and had risen to heaven in a cloud.[66] He now sat in heaven as he had described himself in his vision—on a "throne of power in the angelic council." Eventually he would return, descending from above with the clouds of heaven, surrounded by angels.[67] The time would then have come for the overthrow of the fourth beast—

Rome—and the Messiah would thus fulfill Daniel's vision of the "son of man."

THE MESSIAH OF QUMRAN AND JESUS

The exact date of Jesus' birth is not known. It is thought that he was born in 6 BCE,[68] that is to say, close to the time that the Messiah of Qumran died. One therefore cannot suppose that there was any personal contact between this Messiah and Jesus. At the same time, I believe that the figure of the Qumranic Messiah and the messianic ideology connected with him had a profound influence on Jesus and the development of Christian messianism.

Jesus came from Galilee. Certain aspects of his personality can be explained by the spiritual characteristics of the environment in which he grew up.[69] In his role as a miracle worker and healer of the sick, Jesus resembled the Galilean Hasidim of his period, who also engaged in such activities.[70] Jesus' moral sensitivity likewise has its parallel in the tales about the Galilean Hasidim and in the sayings of Hillel.[71] Jesus' parables were also of a kind that was usual for his time and place.[72] However, his messianism—the most important element of Jesus' personality as described in the New Testament—cannot be explained in terms of the Galilean traditions. The Galilean Hasidim were not messianic leaders, and there is not a single tradition associating them with phenomena of this kind.

If we wish to understand Jesus' messianism, we must realize that in addition to the religious and spiritual characteristics that he acquired from his native locality and from the education he received in his youth, he was also influenced in his later years by another religious tradition, from whom he received his messianic doctrine. I now wish to demonstrate that Jesus' messianic image was formed by an encounter with those who maintained the legacy of the Messiah of Qumran.[73]

There is no reason for us to concern ourselves with the miracles performed by Jesus, his parables, or his moral teachings. None of these has any connection with the legacy of Qumran, and we have noted that these grew out of Galilean and Hillelian traditions. We must focus our attention on the Christology of Jesus—that is, his messianic characteristics as described in the Gospels.

THE MESSIANIC SECRET

After Jesus heard the voice from heaven while being baptized by John, he kept the knowledge of his messianic mission to himself and did not reveal it to anyone. The first occasion on which Jesus revealed it to his disciples is recorded in the Gospel of Mark (8:27, 29–31):[74]

> He asked his disciples, "Who do you say that I am?"
> Peter answered him, "You are the Messiah!"
> And he charged them to tell no one about him.
> And he began to teach them that the son of man must suffer many things, and be rejected by the elders and the chief priests and the scribes, and be killed, and after three days rise again.

This story raises a number of questions: Did Jesus see himself as the "son of man"? If so, why did he speak of the "son of man" in the third person? Was Jesus capable of foreseeing his rejection, death, and resurrection?

As we have seen, the dominant tendency in New Testament studies for more than a hundred years has been to deny the historical authenticity of this story. Jesus, it is claimed, did not regard himself as the Messiah and was not recognized as such by his disciples. He was unable to foresee his suffering, death, and resurrection, and this prediction was consequently ascribed to him at a later date. In Bultmann's words: "The scene of *Peter's Confession* is no counter-evidence—on the contrary! For it is an Easter-story projected backward into Jesus' life time."[75] Bultmann argues that all of Jesus predictions of his future passion and resurrection are later fabrications, since "the idea of a suffering, dying and rising Messiah or son of Man was unknown to Judaism."[76]

A similar view has been expressed more recently by G. Vermes, a prominent scholar of the Dead Sea Scrolls and the New Testament, who writes: "[N]either the suffering of the Messiah, nor his death and resurrection, appear to be part of the faith of first-century Judaism."[77]

Our study has revealed that this verdict is only partly true. It does indeed apply to the majority of Jews at the beginning of the first century CE, but not to the disciples of the Qumranic Messiah. This group responded to the trauma of the year 4 BCE by creating a catastrophic model of messianism based on verses of the Bible. The members believed that the suffering, death, and resurrection of the Messiah were a necessary basis for the process of redemption.

During his lifetime the Messiah of Qumran had described himself as a combination of the "son of man," who sits in heaven on a mighty throne, and the "suffering servant," who bears upon himself all sorrows. As we have seen, this Messiah called upon himself the words of Isaiah 53: "despised and rejected by men."

We have here clear evidence that the idea of a suffering Messiah already existed one generation before Jesus.

According to Hystaspes, the resurrection of the great prophet whom we have identified as the Messiah of Qumran took place "after the third day."[78] As we have noted, the belief in the Messiah's resurrection after three days was bound up with the fact that for three days the Romans forbade burial of his body, which was left in the street for all to see.

Jesus expected the fate of the "son of man" to be similar to that of the Messiah of Qumran. He predicted that the "son of man" would be killed, just as the Qumranic Messiah had been killed by the Roman soldiers. And he expected that the "son of man" would rise after three days, just as it was believed that the Messiah of Qumran had been resurrected "after the third day."[79]

THE NIGHT AT GETHSEMANE

Jesus' messianic mission was therefore a journey towards a known suffering and death. According to the idea he received from the Qumranic Messiah's disciples, the suffering and death of the Messiah formed an inseparable part of the messianic destiny. For someone to take such a mission upon himself was naturally very difficult, and it would seem that Jesus' way of speaking about himself in the third person as the "son of man" reflected that fact.

The difficulty of this mission is dramatically described in the story of the last night of Jesus' life. After the Last Supper, Jesus went to the Garden of Gethsemane with his disciples. There he fell into a deep depression:

> And he took with him Peter and James and John, and began
> to be greatly distressed and troubled.

And he said to them, "My soul is very sorrowful, even to
   death; remain here and watch."
And going a little farther, he fell on the ground and prayed
   that, if it were possible, the hour might pass from him.
And he said, "Abba, Father, all things are possible to thee;
   remove this cup from me; yet not what I will, but what
   thou wilt." (Mark 14:33–36)[80]

The inner struggle in Jesus' soul had now reached its climax.
Jesus felt that the time had come to fulfill his messianic mission—
one that would surely mean suffering and death. As his will to live
rebelled against such a fearful destiny, he begged his almighty
Father to revoke this harsh decree. Yet he nevertheless resigned
himself to what he believed to be the divine decision, setting
aside his own will for that of God. He was thus going to follow
the path of his predecessor, the "suffering servant" of the Dead
Sea Scrolls.

CHAPTER THREE

Another Paraclete

In this chapter, I wish to suggest a historical identity for the Messiah before Jesus.

The argument of this chapter is based on an assumption accepted by most scholars of the Dead Sea literature, though not by all. I refer to the identification of the people of Qumran with the Essenes, known to us from the writings of Josephus Flavius and the Jewish philosopher Philo of Alexandria.[1] Despite the high degree of probability, in my opinion, that this assumption is correct, it is not indisputable fact. The discussion that follows therefore depends on the reasonableness of this assumption.

The identity I am proposing for the Qumran Messiah is also only a hypothesis. The fragmentary, problematic character of the sources relating to the historical personality I am seeking to identify as the Qumran Messiah prevents us from being too categorical.

I wish to point out, however, that the validity of the main

thesis of this book does not depend on acceptance of the assumptions underlying this chapter. My claim that the combination of divinity and suffering, which is clearly found in the messianic hymn, influenced the emergence of Christianity still stands, even if we do not succeed in identifying the hero of the hymns and the exact historical reasons for the rise of the messianic movement he headed. Those who reject the identification of the Qumran sect with the Essenes and thus would deny the historical identity of the Messiah based on that assumption will still have to grapple with the main thesis of this book.

MENAHEM, THE KING'S BELOVED

The first of the two messianic hymns inserted in the Thanksgivings Scroll constitutes a sort of self-portrait of the messianic hero. The vicissitudes of time have damaged this picture: parts of it are missing and its colors have faded. But if we wish to identify this messianic hero, we have to take a careful look at the portrait fragments contained in the hymn.

Significant information about the leader may be gleaned from the way he describes his closeness to God and his place among the angels. He portrays himself as "the beloved of the king."[2] He adds: "my glory [shall be reckoned] with the sons of the king."[3] These, of course, are metaphorical expressions: the king, in this context, is God,[4] and the king's sons are the angels. However, the very fact that such expressions are used requires explanation: the title "the beloved of the king" is an unusual way to describe one's relationship to God,[5] and the description of the angels as the king's sons is unprecedented.[6] Why did the messianic hero choose to use such unusual expressions? It is surely not unreasonable to suppose that these metaphors reflect the life experience of the protagonist of the hymns. It seems that the messianic leader belonged to the court of an earthly king. At the court that he frequented were people who were considered the king's friends, and the circle of these friends also included the king's sons.

Additional information is provided by the hero's boastful declaration: "Who can associate with me and thus compare with my judgment?"[7]

With this information we can construct a kind of profile of the messianic leader: we assume that he was the friend of a king, was in contact with the king's sons, and had judicial functions.

We might begin our investigation into the identity of the messianic leader by examining his friendship with the king. Who was the king in question?

King Herod emulated the ways of the Hellenistic rulers of his time. Like them, he had at his court a group of counselors and senior officials known as "friends" or "beloveds,"[8] some of whom he appointed as advisors to his sons.[9] The friends also served as judges in special courts set up by Herod.[10] Thus, Herod's court could be the source of the metaphors used in the messianic hymn from Qumran.

What was the nature of Herod's relationship with the members of the Qumran sect? Do we know of any member of the sect who could have been counted among his court visitors?

Most scholars of the Dead Sea Scrolls accept that the Qumran sect can be identified with the Essenes. In his writings Josephus describes the sympathy and respect that Herod had for the Essenes. The reason for this sympathy, he said, was the special relationship that Herod had developed with Menahem the Essene. We will first consider the story as Josephus tells it:

> It is, however, proper to explain what reason Herod had for holding the Essenes in honour and for having a higher opinion of them than was consistent with their merely human nature. For such an explanation is not out of place in a work of history, since it will at the same time show what the general opinion of these men was.
>
> There was a certain Essene named Menahem, whose virtue was attested in his whole conduct of life and especially in his having from God a foreknowledge of the future. This man had once observed Herod, then still a boy, going to his teacher, and greeted him as "king of the Jews." Thereupon Herod, who thought that the man either did not know who he was, or was teasing him, reminded him that he was only a private citizen. Menahem, however, gently smiled and slapped him on the backside, saying, "Nevertheless, you will be king and you will rule the realm happily, for you have been found worthy of this by God. And you shall remember the blows given by Menahem, so that they, too, may be for you a symbol of how one's fortune can change. For the best attitude for you to take would be to love justice and piety towards God and mildness toward your citizens. But I know that you will not be such a person, since I understand the whole situation. Now you will be singled out for such good fortune as no other man has had, and you will enjoy eternal glory, but you will forget piety and justice. This, however, cannot escape the notice of God, and at the close of your life His wrath will show that He is mindful of these things." At the moment Herod paid very little attention to his words, for he was quite lacking in such hopes, but after gradually being

advanced to kingship and good fortune, when he was at the
height of his power, he sent for Menahem and questioned
him about the length of time he would reign. Menahem said
nothing at all. In the face of his silence, Herod asked further
whether he had ten years more to reign, and the other re-
plied that he had twenty or even thirty, but he did not set
a limit to the appointed time. Herod, however, was satisfied
even with this answer and dismissed Menahem with a friendly
gesture. And from that time on he continued to hold all Essenes in honour. Now we have seen fit to report these things
to our readers, however incredible they may seem, and to
reveal what has taken place among us because many of these
men have indeed been vouchsafed a knowledge of divine
things because of their virtue.[11]

This story is undoubtedly something of a legend, like the
other stories told by Josephus about the Essenes' capacities to
predict the fate of rulers.[12] At the same time, Menahem's prophecy is used here as evidence of Herod's election by God.[13] Although we do not have to accept the story in its entirety as lit-
eral, historical truth, we can learn from Josephus that Herod
respected the Essenes and brought them close to him, and that
he had special ties of friendship with Menahem the Essene. On
the basis of Josephus's account, we can identify "the king's friend,"
the protagonist of the messianic hymns, as this Menahem.

The favor Herod showed to the Essene sect under the leadership of Menahem should be seen in the light of his policies towards the Jewish society of his time. Herod belonged to a family
of Idumean extraction and as such lacked roots in the Jewish
community. He had been appointed king of Judea by the Roman
Senate and ruled by favor of the Romans. Herod ousted from

office the Hasmoneans, who had ruled in Israel for more than a hundred years. The Sadducees—the priestly aristocracy who had supported the Hasmoneans—were hostile to Herod. He therefore had to look to other elements of Jewish society in order to gain support for himself and his regime. He found this support in moderate Pharisee circles under the leadership of Hillel and in the Jews of the diaspora.[14] The Essenes, the people of the Qumran sect, had been persecuted by the Hasmoneans and so were also possible allies from Herod's viewpoint.[15]

The second messianic hymn, as we have seen, describes a marvelous period in which wickedness and oppression had disappeared from the land and been replaced by light and joy, peace and conciliation:

> [. . . wickedness perishes . . .]
> the oppressor ceases with indignation]
> light appears, and j[oy pours forth];
> grief [disappears], and groaning flees; peace appears, terror
>   ceases.[16]

This description appears to reflect the profound change that had taken place in the position of the Qumran sect in the time of Herod. From the point of view of the people of Qumran, the fate that had overtaken their Hasmonean enemies was a sign of the beginning of redemption. The Hasmonean rulers had been hostile to them, tyrannizing over them and even attempting to kill their founder, the "teacher of righteousness." In the period of Hasmonean rule they had had to abandon their place of residence and settle in the desert region near the Dead Sea. Herod, who had driven the Hasmoneans from office, respected the Essenes and especially their leader, Menahem; *they* were the ones who now enjoyed honor and prestige. Against this background one can understand the meaning of the following words from the second hymn:

> raising up those who stumble
> but casting down the lofty assemblies of the eternally proud.

The proud who were cast down were the members of the Hasmonean aristocracy, and the stumblers who were raised were the members of the Qumran sect.

Menahem's relationship with Rome and its culture was two-faceted. On the one hand, he was influenced by the Roman culture of his period, as we will discuss at length in appendix B. At the same time, like all the members of his community, he nurtured a deep hatred for the Romans, whom the Essenes saw as conquerors and oppressors. The fact that Menahem was one of the "friends" of Herod, who ruled by favor of the Romans, caused him to live a double existence. Yet this way of living was nothing new for Menahem and his followers. In the Manual of Discipline from Qumran—a description of the laws and regulations that governed the behavior of the members of the sect—we find the following:

> These are the rules for the instructor in those times with respect to his loving and hating: Everlasting hatred for the men of perdition in spirit of secrecy . . . and meekness before him who lords it over him; to be a man zealous for the ordinance and its time, for the day of vengeance.[17]

These are instructions for living a double life! A member of the sect must behave humbly, "like a slave before his master,"[18] toward the "men of perdition" who "lord it over him," but in the secrecy of his heart he must hate these men and await the day of vengeance when he will openly wage war against them. The pacifism of the Essenes was only a provisional pacifism and would end on the day of vengeance.[19] However, as we have tried to show with the imaginary reconstruction at the beginning of the book, this general injunction to live a double life was apparently exemplified in a special way and to an exceptional degree in the life of "the king's friend," Menahem.

THE EXCOMMUNICATION

The death of King Herod in 4 BCE and the revolt that took place in the country at that time permitted Menahem to cease living his double life and reveal his messianic secret to the general public.

We learn of the circumstances in which this secret was revealed from rabbinic sources. The oldest collection of rabbinic literature, the Mishna, mentions[20] five pairs of religious leaders who succeeded one another during the period from the Hasmonean rebellion (167 BCE) to the time of Herod.[21] Hillel and Menahem were named as the pair active in the time of Herod. The Mishna adds: "Menahem went out, and Shammai came in."

What do the rabbinic sources have to say about the Menahem who was active in the time of Herod and why he "went out"? Menahem is undoubtedly an exceptional figure in rabbinic literature. In all the extensive rabbinic writings not a single law or statement was made in his name. In the tractate Avot a list of sages is given in order of generations, but the name Menahem does not appear in that list at all.[22] It would thus seem that Menahem was not one of the Pharisaic sages but belonged to one of the

opposing sects.[23] For that reason, many scholars from the six-
teenth century until the present, have identified the Menahem
referred to in the rabbinic sources with Menahem the Essene
mentioned in Josephus.[24] The rabbinic sources say that Menahem
was a member of the king's court,[25] which corresponds to what
we are told about Menahem the Essene in Josephus.

The Jerusalem Talmud quotes the statement "Menahem went
out" from the Mishna and asks, "Where did he go?" It answers:

> Some say he went from one way of behaving to another
> and some say he turned round and left;
> he and eighty pairs of Torah scholars clad in golden *tirki*[26]
> [armor],[27]
> whose faces went black as pots
> because they told them,
> "Write on a bull's horns that you have no part in the God
> of Israel."[28]

This description is a verbal photograph of an extraordinary
event.[29] Menahem is surrounded by a hundred and sixty disciples
clad in golden—that is, shining—armor.[30] Opposite Menahem
and his disciples stands another group, who are excommunicat-
ing them. The excommunicators tell Menahem and his disciples
that they are rejected from the Jewish people. They say: "Write
on a bull's horns that you have no part in the God of Israel."[31]
Menahem does not answer but turns around and goes out with
his disciples in silence and disgrace—their faces "black as pots."

Menahem's disciples are described in this passage as wearing
coats of armor. At the time he was excommunicated, Menahem
was the leader of a military group with revolutionary ambi-
tions.[32] In view of the friendship between Menahem and Herod,

it is hard to believe that Menahem would have taken part in a revolt during the king's lifetime. It would seem, rather, that the event described in the Jerusalem Talmud was connected with the revolt that took place after Herod's death in 4 BCE.

Why was Menahem excommunicated at the time of the revolt?

The only mention of Menahem in the Mishna is in chapter two of the tractate Hagiga. This chapter opens with a famous prohibition on investigating—especially in public—certain secret areas of religious knowledge:

> The forbidden degrees may not be expounded before three
>   persons,
> nor the story of the creation before two,
> nor the chapter of the chariot before one alone,
> unless he is a Sage that understands his own knowledge.
> Whoever gives his mind to four things,
> it were better if he had not come into the world—
> what is above,
> what is beneath,
> what was beforetime
> and what will be hereafter.
> And whosoever takes no thought for the honor of his Maker,
> it were better for him if he had not come into the world.

In this passage one is totally forbidden to concern oneself with certain areas of knowledge—"what is above, what is below, what was beforetime, and what will be hereafter"—and restrictions are placed on publicly discussing the secrets of the creation or attempting a description of the seat of God in heaven—"the chapter of the chariot."[33] The Mishna ends with a sharp condemnation of anyone who fails to consider God's honor.

Scholars have had difficulty understanding how this discussion fits into the tractate Hagiga. Each tractate deals with a certain topic. The tractate Hagiga deals with matters connected to the ceremonies that took place in the Temple during festivals. The prohibition against slighting God's honor by concerning oneself with the secrets of the creation or the seat of God in heaven has no connection with this subject. I believe that the solution to this problem, which has troubled commentators on the Mishna for many centuries,[34] lies with the figure of Menahem.

Significantly, the only mention of Menahem in the Mishna occurs immediately after the remarks on the wickedness of slighting God's honor. The protagonist of the messianic hymns, whom we have identified with Menahem, describes himself as sitting in the heavens on a "throne of power" in the midst of a "council" of angels. He even dares to ask, "Who is like me among the angels?" There is no doubt that from the point of view of the Sages, the admonition: "whosoever takes no thought for the honor of his Maker, it is better for him if he had not come into the world" most definitely applied to him. The remarks on the wickedness of slighting God's honor were included in the tractate Hagiga precisely in order to explain Menahem's "going out." Menahem "went out"[35] because he failed to consider the honor of his Maker. This also explains the observation in the Talmud that Menahem "went forth into evil courses."[36]

The picture of the excommunication reported in the Jerusalem Talmud now becomes clearer. During Herod's reign Menahem was unable to publicly declare his messianic aspirations, as it would have been considered rebellion against the king, but after Herod's death he thought that the time had come to publicly proclaim his messiahship. He and his disciples believed that the time of the eschatological "war between the Sons of Light and the Sons of Darkness," for which they had prepared for so many years, had finally arrived. Menahem would have liked to have made the Pharisaic sages his partners in this war. This would have been in keeping with the desire prevailing in the sect at that period to seek the collaboration of the people of Israel as a whole.[37] Menahem stood at the head of his armor-clad disciples, facing the Pharisee Sages, and told them of his messianic aspirations and his military plans. Perhaps in order to strengthen his claims to the messiahship, he publicly described his mystical experience of sitting in heaven on a "throne of power." What until then had been a "messianic secret" preserved within the closed circle of the Qumran sect was now publicly proclaimed. But Menahem's hope was disappointed. The Pharisee Sages rejected him and would not accept his messianic pretensions. The Sages thought his claim that he had sat on a "throne of power" in heaven was blasphemy and consequently excommunicated him and his disciples, declaring them to have "no part in the God of Israel." Crushed by his disappointment, Menahem fell silent and did not answer. He turned away and left shamefacedly with his disciples.

In the Midrash to the Song of Songs, the story of Menahem's exit begins as follows: "In the days of Menahem and Hillel, when there was a dispute between them and Menahem went out."[38] Hillel was the leader of the group of Sages who excommunicated Menahem.[39]

It is instructive to compare the figures of Hillel and Menahem, who lived and worked in the same period. Hillel was the leader of the Pharisees, and Menahem the leader of the Essenes.

Quite surprisingly, there is a point of similarity between the two leaders. We have seen how Menahem described his great proximity to God and was not afraid to express his privileged position by paraphrasing a verse from the Bible relating to God: "Who is like me among the angels?" Remarkably, Hillel also used passages in the Bible relating to God in order to describe his status. He applied to himself the words of Exodus 20:24: "In every place where I cause my name to be remembered, I will come to you and bless you,"[40] as well as a passage from the Psalms: "Who is like the Lord our God, who is seated on high, who looks far down upon the heavens and the earth?"[41] On the face of it, Hillel's audacity was no less great than Menahem's. If this was so, why did Hillel and his colleagues excommunicate Menahem?

Along with the similarities there was in fact a significant difference between Menahem and Hillel. After his mystical experience Menahem regarded himself as a person raised above others. He no longer considered himself a being of flesh and blood, as is shown by his statement, "[My] desi[re] is not of the flesh." This denial of physicality is in keeping with his description of himself sitting in the heavens on a "throne of power" in the congregation of the angels. He was a messianic figure who claimed to be quasi-divine. This quasi-divinity distinguished him from all other human beings and formed the basis of his messianic claims.

The figure of Menahem corresponds closely to the figure of the sectarian leader described by Gershom Scholem:

> In the history of religion we frequently encounter types
> of individuals known as "pneumatics" or "spiritualists." . . .
> These terms did not refer to just anyone who may have had
> occasion in the course of his life to be "moved by the spirit";
> rather, they applied only to those few who abode in the

"palace of the king," that is, who lived in continual communion with a spiritual realm through whose gates they had
passed. . . . One so favored was in certain respects no longer
considered to be subject to the laws of everyday reality, having realized within himself the hidden world of divine light.
Naturally, spiritualistic types of this sort have always regarded themselves as forming a group apart, and hence the
special sense of their own "superiority" by which they are
characterized. . . . Here, then, we have all the prerequisites
for the sectarian disposition, for the sect serves the *illuminati*
as both a rallying point for their own kind and a refuge
from the incomprehension of the carnal and unenlightened
masses.[42]

Hillel, on the other hand, had no messianic pretensions. The
source of Hillel's spiritual audacity was his awareness of the religious implications of the creation of human beings in the image
of God. This is shown by the following story:

When Hillel went to a place, people would say to him:
  Where are you going?
  I am going to fulfill a commandment.
  Which commandment, Hillel?
  I am going to the toilet.
  But this is a commandment?
  He answered: *Yes, it is, so that the body may not deteriorate.*

Or again:
  Where are you going, Hillel?
  I am going to fulfill a commandment.
  Which commandment, Hillel?
  I am going to the baths.

But is this a commandment?
He answered: *Yes, it is, in order to clean the body.*

> Know, then, that this is a fact, because if the government
> gives an annual pension to the official in charge of polishing
> and buffing the statues which stand in the palaces of kings
> and if even further he is elevated to the rank of the great men
> of the kingdom, then all the more so for those of us who
> were created in the image and likeness.[43]

In Hillel's view, human beings owed their lofty status to the
fact that they were created in God's image. The Messiah of Qumran rejected his physicality by saying: "[My] desi[re] is not of
the flesh."[44] Hillel accepted the body and its needs.[45] If the physical body as the image of God was the foundation of human dig-
nity, this obviously applied to everyone without exception. Thus,
Hillel never claimed any special position in relation to others.[46]

The background for Hillel's words was the worship of images
of the Roman emperor, or in other words, the imperial cult that
was emerging in the time of Augustus. Both Hillel and Menahem
lived under the reign of Herod, who was one of the supporters
and disseminators of this cult.[47] Both of them reflected the spirit
of their time, but there was a decisive difference in the ways that
they did so. The Messiah, influenced by Augustus's propaganda,
appropriated for himself the concept of a redeemer with divine
attributes. Hillel, on the other hand, reacted to the imperial cult
by stressing the principle that human beings are created in the
image of the divine. Every person, he taught, is partly divine because that person is made in the image of God.[48]

Once one has grasped the difference between the viewpoints
of Hillel and Menahem, the background to the excommunication

becomes intelligible. Menahem claimed that he had been raised above the rest of humanity and that his physical nature had been eliminated. He described himself as sitting on the throne of God in heaven. For Hillel and his colleagues, this was an insult to God's honor, a wicked attempt to blur the distinction between the creator and his creation. Menahem, they thought, was one of those who "takes no thought for the honor of his Maker," for whom "it were better . . . if he had not come into the world." Thus, Hillel and his colleagues had no choice but to excommunicate Menahem and his disciples clad in shining armor.

THE REVOLT AND THE SLAYING OF MENAHEM

The talmudic sources do not relate the military actions of Menahem and his hundred and sixty disciples. Josephus, however, tells us that among those who took part in the revolt were people close to King Herod,[49] and so the participation of Menahem, "the king's friend," would not be unimaginable. The role of Menahem as a messianic leader corresponds to what we know about the leaders of the revolt:

> The Jewish revolt after Herod's death had no one leader and no unified command. It was essentially a series of spontaneous risings which broke out independently of one another in various parts of the country. . . . The leaders of these risings . . . adopted royal titles. It may be conjectured that this phenomenon was linked with eschatological expectations, such as brought individual messianic figures to prominence.[50]

The seeds of the revolt had already been sown during Herod's last days. When Herod was ailing and near death, two Pharisaic scholars in Jerusalem, Judah and Mattathias, urged their disciples to remove the golden eagle that Herod had placed over the gate of the Temple, arguing that representations of living creatures were forbidden according to Jewish law. By erecting the eagle Herod had been trying to please the Romans, for whom the eagle was a major symbol. Thus the opposition to the eagle must be seen as a mixture of political and religious zealotry. When there was a rumor that Herod had died, the disciples of Judah and Mattathias went out and destroyed the eagle with axes. The rumor, however, was false: Herod was not yet dead; when he heard about the destruction of the eagle, he ordered Mattathias and some of his disciples to be burnt.[51]

Herod died a short time afterwards, and his son Archelaus succeeded him on the throne. Thousands of pilgrims had gathered in Jerusalem for the festival of Passover. The disciples of Mattathias and Judah stirred up the people against Archelaus. The new king sent his cavalry against the crowds and three thousand people were killed. After the festival Archelaus left for Rome, and the revolt now erupted with full force.[52] The rebels rose up against Archelaus's supporters and against the Roman soldiers stationed in the Tower of Phasael near the royal palace. The soldiers poured out of the tower and assailed the rebels. Then the rebels went up onto the roof of the chambers of the Temple and from there threw stones and catapulted missiles on the Romans. In response, the Roman soldiers set fire to the chambers, which immediately went up in flames, causing the death of many of the rebels. The Romans then entered the court-yard of the Temple and pillaged the Temple treasury.[53]

This is the background to what we read at the beginning of chapter 11 of the Book of Revelation: "But do not measure the court outside the temple; leave that out, for it is given over to the nations."

And what of the two witnesses—the two "olive trees"—who appear a little later in the same chapter?

> And when they have finished their testimony, the beast that
>   ascends from the abyss will make war upon them and con-
>   quer them and kill them.
> And their dead bodies will lie in the street of the great
>   city . . . where also our Lord was crucified. (Rev. 11:7–8)

We see that the bodies of two witnesses—two messianic leaders killed by the Roman soldiers—lay in the streets of Jerusalem.[54] Of these two messianic witnesses it is written in this chapter: "These are the two olive-trees and the two lampstands which stand before the Lord of the earth" (Rev. 11:4). Menahem was probably one of these two messianic witnesses.

THE PARACLETE

We have seen that from start to finish, Jesus' messianic vocation bears the imprint of Menahem's messianism. In this section I demonstrate that the Gospel of John, in particular, preserves a tradition that reflects the line of continuity from Menahem to Jesus. This tradition is the mysterious concept of the Paraclete.

According to the Gospel of John, at the time of the Last Supper Jesus promised his disciples that he would ask the Father— that is, God—to send them "another Paraclete." The Paraclete, which is also described as the "Holy Spirit" and the "spirit of truth," would lead them to the truth and show them "things to come."[55] Similarly, the Paraclete would "convince the world concerning sin and righteousness and judgment."[56] In view of these statements, the Paraclete could be described as a teacher, a prophet who foretells the future, and a revealer of truths. Jesus told his disciples that the Paraclete would appear only if and when he left the world.[57] We can conclude from this that Jesus regarded the wondrous figure of the Paraclete as someone who would replace him.

Two questions arise here. The first is: Why was this wondrous figure called the "Paraclete"? Moreover, according to John (14:16), Jesus described this figure as *another* Paraclete. He thus appears to have regarded himself as a Paraclete.[58] So the second question is: Why should Jesus have described himself this way?

First of all, we must examine the meaning of the word *paraclete* in the period when the Gospel was written. The primary meaning of this word was connected with courts of law. According to Greek sources and according to the rabbinic literature, a paraclete was the counsel for the defense in a trial,[59] but nothing in the Gospel of John describing the functions of the Paraclete suggests a judicial function of this kind.[60] In ancient translations of the Bible the word *paraclete* and the verbs connected with it served as a translation for the Hebrew verb *nahem* (to comfort) and the nouns *menahem, menahemim* (comforter, comforters).[61] For this reason the Church Fathers described the Paraclete as someone who comforts mourners.[62] But this interpretation does not suit the figure described in John's Gospel either, as comforting mourners is not listed among the functions of the Paraclete.[63] The attempt to find Gnostic analogies to the figure of the Paraclete[64] is not convincing either.[65]

The discovery of the Dead Sea Scrolls, however, has shed new light on the Paraclete. The Gospel of John describes the Paraclete as the "spirit of truth" (14:17). Even before the discovery of these scrolls, scholars drew attention to the Jewish origins of this expression.[66] From the scrolls it became apparent that the "spirit of truth" was a central concept in the theology of the people of Qumran. It represented the positive pole in the Qumranic dualistic vision of light and darkness, truth and falsehood.[67] A number of scholars have consequently thought that the figure of the Paraclete in John is bound up with the Dead Sea Scrolls' philosophy.[68]

In light of our findings in this book, the connection between the figure of the Paraclete and the Essenes should be stressed further. As we said, the word *paraclete* in ancient translations of the Bible was used to render the Hebrew term *menahem*.[69] "Paraclete" in the Gospel of John is thus, in my opinion, a translation of the name of the Essene Messiah, *Menahem*.[70] As we know, the name of Julius Caesar, the first ruler of the Roman Empire, became the title of the Roman rulers who followed him, who were all called "Caesar." Similarly, the name of Menahem, the first of the Jewish messiahs, came to represent the Messiah as such.[71] The idea that the name of the Messiah is "Menahem" is documented in rabbinic literature.[72] The tradition of the Paraclete in the Gospel of John represents a Christian manifestation of this convention.

When Jesus said that the Father would send "another Paraclete," he revealed that he himself was a Paraclete.[73] These words reflect the idea that Jesus continued Menahem's tradition and was his successor. Jesus said that when he went away, God would send another Paraclete—that is to say, another Menahem. That Paraclete would be a copy of Jesus and he would perform the tasks that Jesus had done in his life.[74] The tradition of the Paraclete in the Gospel of John expresses the unique concept of a *chain* of redeemers.[75] This tradition succinctly expresses the chief claim of this book, which is that Jesus was the heir and successor of the Messiah of Qumran.[76]

According to the Gospel of John, Jesus spoke about the Paraclete at the Last Supper. Christian tradition places the site of the Last Supper on Mount Zion in Jerusalem,[77] which is where Menahem the Essene had lived and worked. It seems that the "upper chamber" in which the Last Supper was held belonged to one of the Essenes who had stayed on in Jerusalem after the death of their leader.[78] The words of Jesus at the Last Supper also demonstrate the close connection that existed between Jesus and Menahem.

Jesus did see himself as the Messiah. He indeed foresaw his suffering and death. His vision of his future rejection, death, and resurrection was based on the life and death of his predecessor. Hence, we may say that Jesus really was "another Paraclete"—a second Menahem.

Postscript

In 70 CE, about forty years after Jesus' death, the Temple in Jerusalem was destroyed. In the Jerusalem Talmud, there is a legend about something that took place on the day of the destruction:

> A Jew was ploughing and his cow was lowing as he went.
> An Arab who passed by heard it, and said: "Son of the Jews, release your cow and abandon your plough, for the Temple has been destroyed."
> The ox lowed again, and the Arab said: "Son of the Jews, tie up your cow and tie up your plough, for King Messiah has been born."
> The Jew asked: "What is his name?"
> The other answered: "Menahem."
> The Jew asked: "What is his father's name?"
> The other answered: "Hezekiah."
> The Jew asked: "Where is he from?"
> The other answered: "From the dwelling place of the King, Bethlehem in Judah."

The Jew sold his cow and his plough and became a seller of
  infants' swaddling clothes.

He went in and out of one town after another until he came
  to that town, and all the women bought from him, but
  Menahem's mother did not buy.

He heard the women say: "Mother of Menahem, mother of
  Menahem, come and buy for your son!"

She told him: "I should like to strangle my son Menahem,[1]
  for on the day he was born, the Temple was destroyed."

He told her: "We are sure that just as he marked its destruction, so he shall build it once more."

She said: "I have no money."

He said: "No matter, come and buy, and if you have no
  money today, after some days I shall come and collect it."

After some days, he came back to the town, and asked her:
  "How is the child?"

She said: "After you saw me, a mighty wind came and
  snatched him out of my hands."[2]

Here the Messiah is called Menahem, son of Hezekiah.[3] The
figure of Menahem in this story combines various elements
known to us from the traditions concerning the Essene Messiah
and Jesus of Nazareth. Menahem, the son of Hezekiah, resembles
the Essene Messiah not only in his name but also in his destiny.
A wind snatched this Menahem out of his mother's hands.[4] Similarly, in the Oracle of Hystaspes it is said that the great prophet,
whom we have identified as Menahem, was snatched away and
taken up to heaven.

One element that Jesus and Menahem, son of Hezekiah, have
in common is their place of birth, Bethlehem.[5] Further, the Gospel of Matthew says that the Magi came from far away to Jesus'

birthplace in Bethlehem and gave his mother gifts.[6] In a similar way, the Jew in the story from the Jerusalem Talmud wandered from place to place until he found the Messiah's mother in Bethlehem and gave her swaddling clothes as a present.[7] According to Matthew, Herod threatened the life of the infant Messiah; in the story in the Jerusalem Talmud, it was the Messiah's mother who wanted to kill him.[8]

As a child, Menahem, son of Hezekiah, was a rejected figure. His mother rejected him and sought his death because he was born on the day the Temple was destroyed. At the same time, this rejected Messiah was the true Messiah. The wind carried him to heaven, but he would eventually return and be revealed as Israel's redeemer. Referring to the destroyed Temple, the Jew said to Menahem's mother: "We are sure that just as he marked its destruction, so he shall build it once more." In this way, the talmudic legend adopted the idea of a catastrophic messianism developed by the disciples of Menahem the Essene: the destruction was a necessary stage in the redemptive process. It is as if the legend of the rejected Messiah, Menahem, the son of Hezekiah, expresses a willingness on the part of the rabbinic tradition to revoke the excommunication of Menahem the Essene Messiah and recognize his important role in the process of redemption.[9] This development reached its culmination in the midrashic tradition concerning the Messiah, son of Joseph, who was killed in the war of redemption and was destined to be resurrected.[10] This tradition was a reflection of the historical story of Menahem the Essene Messiah.[11] The figure of Menahem, the hero of our book, was the foundation of the Jewish messianic myth, just as he served as the inspiration for the messianism of Jesus of Nazareth.

The Messianic Hymns

THE MANUSCRIPTS

The messianic hymns exist in two parallel versions.[1] The two versions are similar in character, but at the same time, each one has its own particular features. Version 1 of the hymns is found in three different manuscripts: 4QHe; 4QHa frg. 7; and 1QHa col. 26; while version 2 is to be found in a single manuscript, 4Q491 frg. 11, col. 1. In both versions there is a hymn written in the first person in which the speaker praises himself. This hymn, which scholars call the Self-Glorification Hymn, is followed in both versions by a second hymn that calls on the members of the community to offer praise to God.

HYMN 1, VERSION 1

The main documentation of version 1 of the first hymn is to be found in two fragments of 4QHe. In the first fragment, we read:[2]

1 the holy [council]. Wh[o
2 has been rejected [of men] like me?
3 compares to my teaching.
4 Who is like me among the angels?
5 who could measure the [flow] of my lips? Who
6 am the beloved of the king, a companion of the ho[
7 none can compare, for I [
8 with gold <I> will cro[wn

And in the second fragment, we read:

1 who] has been despised like [me?
2 compares to m[e in enduring] evil?
3] I sit [

A third fragment only contains part of a single word.[3]

Although these texts are very fragmented, we can turn for help to the other manuscripts of version 1, in which parallel expressions are sometimes preserved in a more complete form. Parallel expressions in version 2 are also helpful for our purpose. On the basis of all this direct and indirect evidence, we can attempt to reconstruct version 1 of hymn 1 as follows:[4]

1 [. . . I shall be r]eckon[ed with the angels, my dwelling is in] the holy[5]
2 [council.] Wh[o . . . And who] has been despised like [me? And who]
3 has been rejected [of men][6] like me? [And who] compares to m[e in enduring] evil? [No teaching]
4 compares to my teaching.[7] [For] I sit [. . . in heaven][8]
5 Who is like me among the angels? [Who could cut off my words? And][9]

6   who could measure the [flow] of my lips? Who [can associate with me thus compare with my judgment? [10] I]

7   am the beloved of the king, a companion of the ho[ly ones and none can accompany me. And to my glory] [11]

8   none can compare, for I [. . . Neither]

9   with gold <I> will cro[wn myself, nor with refined gold] [12]

HYMN 1, VERSION 2

The second version of this hymn is preserved in lines 5–11 [13] of document 4Q491 frg. 11, col. 1:

5   [. . . for]ever a throne of power in the angelic council. No king of yore will sit therein, neither will their nobles.[14] [. . . Who can be compared to]

6   [me?] None can compare [to] my glory, and none has been exalted save myself, and none can accompany me. I sit [. . .] in heaven, and none

7   [. . .] I shall be reckoned with the angels, my dwelling is in the holy council. [My] desi[re] is not of the flesh, [for] everything precious to me is in the glory of

8   the holy [hab]itation. [W]ho has been accounted despicable like me, yet who is like me in my glory? Who is [. . .]

9   [. . .] Who has born[e all] afflictions like me? Who compares to me [in enduri]ng evil? No one is like me and no teaching compares

10   [to my teaching]. Who could cut off m[y words]? And who could measure the flow of my speech? Who can associate with me and thus compare with my judgment?

11   [. . . fo]r I am reckoned with the angels, and my glory with the sons of the king. Neither gold nor refined [g]old.

Hymn 2, Version 1

There are also two versions of the second hymn. Let us first look
at version 1,[15] which is preserved in 4QHa frg. 7, col. 1, lines 13–
23, and col. 2, lines 1–14.

Column 1, lines 13–23

13   Sing praise, O beloved ones, sing to the king of

14   [glory, *rejoice* in the congre]gation of God, ring out joy
in the tents of salvation, give praise in the [holy] habi-
tation,

15   [extol] together among the eternal hosts, ascribe greatness
to our God and glory to our king.

16   [Sanc]tify his name with strong lips and mighty tongue,
raise up together your voice

17   [at a]ll times, sound aloud joyful music, rejoice with everlasting joy

18   [un]ceasingly, worship in the common assembly. Bless
the one who wonderfully does majestic deeds and makes
known his strong hand,

19   [se]aling mysteries and revealing hidden things, raising up
those who stumble and those among them who fall

20   [by res]toring the step of those who wait for knowledge,
but casting down the lofty assemblies of the eternally
proud,

21   [confirm]ing mysteries of spl[endor] and establ[ishing]
glorious [mar]vels; [bless] the one who judges with de-
structive wrath

22   [*l* . . .] in loving kindness, righteousness, and in abundant
mercies, favor

23 [. . .] mercy for those who frustrate his great goodness, and a source of

Column 2, lines 1–14

1 [. . .]

2 [. . . <u>and wickedness perishes</u> . . .]

3 [. . . and op]pression [ceases; <u>the oppressor ceases with indignation</u>]

4 deceit [end]s, and there are no witless perversities; light appears, and j[<u>oy pours forth</u>];

5 grief [disappears], and groaning flees; peace appears, terror ceases; a fountain is opened for [<u>eternal</u>] <u>bles[sing</u>]

6 and [for] healing for all times everlasting; iniquity ends, affliction ceases so that there is no more sick[ness; injustice is <u>removed</u>],

7 [<u>and guil</u>]t is <u>no</u> m[<u>ore</u>. Pr]oclaim and say: Great is God who <u>ac[ts wonderfully</u>],

8 for he casts down the haughty spirit so that there is no remnant and lifts up the poor from the dust to [the eternal height],

9 and to the clouds he magnifies him in stature, and [he is] with the heavenly beings in the assembly of the community and *rp* [. . .]

10 wrath for eternal destruction. And those who stumble on earth he lifts up without charge, and [everlasting] mi[ght is with]

11 their step, and eternal joy in their habitations, everlasting glory without ceasing [for ever and ever].

12 Let them say: blessed is God who [wor]ks mighty [m]arvels, acting mightily to make his power appear, [<u>and doing righteously</u>]

13 [in] knowledge to all his creatures and [in] goodness upon
their faces, so that they might know the abundance of his
loving [kindnes̲s̲e̲s̲, and the multitude of]

14 his mercies to all the children of his truth.[16]

HYMN 2, VERSION 2

Version 2 of the second hymn survives in a fragmentary form in
lines 13–16 of 4Q491 frg. 11, col. 1:[17]

13 [. . . Rejoice,] you righteous among the angels [. . .] in
the holy dwelling, hymn [him]

14 [. . . pro]claim the sound of a ringing cry [. . .] in eternal
joy, without [. . .]

15 [. . .] to establish the horn of [his] Mess[iah] [18]

16 [. . .] to make known his power in might [. . .]

THE IDENTITY OF
THE PROTAGONIST OF THE HYMNS

M. Baillet, who published version two of the first hymn in 1982,
thought the speaker of the hymn was the archangel Michael,[19]
but this idea was challenged by M. Smith.[20] Smith rightly argued
that only a man, not an angel, would boast of being among the
angels and of eliminating fleshly desires.[21] He concluded that the
speaker must have been a member of the sect. This person, who
was a teacher, experienced an ascension to the heavens, and this
experience is reflected in the hymn. J. J. Collins agreed with this
view in his original comments on the piece,[22] but in his book on
the messianism of Qumran he changed his opinion and suggested
that the protagonist of the hymn was not in fact a teacher in the

community but the visionary figure of the priest-Messiah or the teacher at the "end of days."[23]

In his most recent comments on the subject, however, Collins admitted that this idea was problematic. Although there are descriptions of future messianic figures in the Dead Sea literature, there is nothing remotely like this hymn written in the first person. Similarly, there is nothing resembling the audacity expressed in this hymn. As Collins says:

> The problem is that nowhere else in the corpus of the scrolls do we find words placed in the mouth of either Messiah, and so there is no parallel for a speech such as we find in 4Q491 by a messianic figure. Neither is there any parallel for such claims by anyone else.[24]

Collins rightly ruled out[25] the possibility that the speaker is the "teacher of righteousness," the founder and original leader of the sect,[26] as the style and content of the hymn are completely different from those of the thanksgiving psalms ascribed to the "teacher of righteousness." He also rightly claimed that the person described here cannot possibly be a composite personality.[27] The style of the hymn and the assertions it contains show that he is a single individual and not a collective figure.[28] Collins thus concluded in his latest discussion of the subject that the identity of the writer remains an unsolved mystery.[29]

Eshel, following the suggestion that Collins made and subsequently rejected, proposed that the speaker of the hymn could in fact have been the priest at the end of days.[30] She thought that the hymn could be compared with the blessing in the Manual of Discipline[31] generally believed to be a benediction on the priest at the end of days.[32]

May you be as an angel of the Presence in the Abode of
     Holiness to the glory of the God of [host . . .
May y]ou attend upon the service in the Temple of the
     Kingdom
and decree destiny in company with the angels of Presence,
in common council [with the Holy Ones for]
everlasting ages and for all the perpetual periods;
for [all] his judgments [are true].
May he make you holy among his people
and an [eternal] light [to illuminate] the world with
     knowledge
and to enlighten the face of the Congregation [with your
     teaching.
May he] crown you as the Holy of Holies.[33]

Eshel pointed out that in both the hymn and the blessing, the
protagonist is described as dwelling among angels and is depicted as a teacher.[34] She thus came to the conclusion that the
statements in the hymn relate to the imaginary figure of the priest
at the end of days, who was the figure described in the blessing.

Is there any basis for this idea?

I think that a careful comparison of the two composi-
tions shows that the differences between them outweigh the
similarities.

In the blessing from the "Manual of Discipline" there are
definite priestly elements. The hero is described as serving in a
royal temple, which would apply to the priests in the Bible described as "servants of the Lord."[35] This hero is depicted as
wearing the crown of the Holy of Holies—a description be-
fitting the High Priest Aaron in the Bible.[36] On the other hand,

in neither version of the hymn is any priestly element associated with the main character.

Moreover, the connection with the angels, which Eshel considered one of the common features of the two works, exists only on a superficial level. In the descriptions in the Bible and the other Dead Sea literature the angels stand before God, who sits in his heavenly temple on a royal throne, and serve him;[37] in this respect the priest in the blessing, who serves God in a royal temple, does indeed resemble the angels. The hero of the hymn, however, does not stand and serve in a royal temple. He sits in heaven on a "throne of power" in the midst of a "council" of angels. He does not resemble a ministering angel so much as a king, or God himself. This is the real significance of the question "Who is like me among the angels?" asked by the hero of the hymn. It really means: "I am higher than all the angels"!

The scene described in the hymn—a man sitting on a throne of power in heaven—is appropriate not for the figure of the High Priest but for that of the king-Messiah. The hero of the hymn calls himself "the king's friend," or in other words, the friend of God. King Solomon was called Yedidya ("God's friend") and was described as having sat on the "throne of God."[38]

In the Bible we find figures who sit on thrones *next to* God. In Psalm 110:1, God invites a king to sit next to Him: "Sit at my right hand till I make your enemies your footstool." We find a similar motif in the Book of Daniel in connection with the wondrous figure of the "son of man," who probably sat on a throne next to God (Daniel 7:9–14).

The speaker of the hymn, as we have seen, depicts himself as a divine personage, asking, "Who is like me among the angels?"

The idea that the Messiah or the king at the end of days is a figure with divine attributes is already found in the Bible. The prophet Isaiah used the expression "mighty God" in this connection (9:5), and Jeremiah said that the king at the end of days would be called "the Lord our righteousness" (23:6).

Apart from the royal-messianic element, there is another important element in this hymn. The speaker describes himself as a person who has suffered. He says:

And who] has been despised like [me? And who]
has been rejected [of men] like me?[39]

Who has born[e all] afflictions like me? Who compares to
me [in enduri]ng evil?[40]

As we have seen, this motif is obviously connected with the "suffering servant" in Isaiah 53, who is "despised and rejected of men, a man of sorrows and acquainted with grief."

The figure described in the hymn combines characteristics of God, the king-Messiah, and the "suffering servant." As noted, some people have proposed that he is a collective image symbolizing the entire people of Israel.[41] From the information given in the second hymn, however, we can deduce that the speaker here is not a collective entity but the leader of the community, for the second hymn makes a clear distinction between the elevation of the leader, described in the singular:

and lifts up the poor from the dust to [the eternal height],
and to the clouds he magnifies him in stature, and [he is] with
the heavenly beings in the assembly of the community.

and the raising up of the whole community, described in the plural:

> And those who stumble on earth he lifts up without charge.[42]

It is interesting to compare the language of the first version of the second hymn with that of the other psalms in the Thanksgivings Scroll. The following lines appear in a psalm in the Thanksgivings Scroll from cave 1:

> to groan the groaning of grief and sighing on the lyre of
> lamentation
> in utter grieving sorrow and bitter lament,
> until the destruction of wickedness, . . . and there will be no
> more pain or affliction to cause sickness,
> and then I will sing upon the lyre of salvation and the harp
> of joy.[43]

The destruction of iniquity and affliction is described here as a future event that will come to pass after the present period of distress. Only then will one be able to "sing upon the lyre of salvation." At present, there is only "grief and sighing on the lyre of lamentation."

In contrast, our hymn speaks of a period in which mourning has vanished and all the signs of redemption are already manifest:

> grief [disappears], and groaning flees; peace appears, terror
> ceases;
> affliction ceases so there is no more sick[ness.[11]

The members of the community are called upon to sing the praises of salvation here and now:

Sing praise, O beloved ones,
ring out joy in the tents of salvation.[45]

One has the impression that the writer of the hymn has taken
the expressions of prayer for future redemption found in the
original thanksgiving psalms[46] and used them to describe the salvation of the community in the present. He has transferred the
language of hope for the future that he found in the Thanksgivings Scroll to the present, in order to express the feelings of the
redeemed sect.[47]

Thus, we may conclude by saying that the two hymns that
were inserted into the Thankgivings Scroll bear witness to a messianic movement that arose within the Qumran community. The
messianic leader of this movement was the speaker of the Self-
Glorification Hymn.

Between Rome and Jerusalem

When Jesus died on the cross, a Roman centurion who stood near him said, "Truly this man was the son of God." [1] According to the Gospel of Luke, the title "son of God" had already been given to Jesus at the annunciation to Mary:

> And, behold, you will conceive in your womb, and bear
>   a son, and you will call his name Jesus.
> He will be great, and he will be called the son of the Most
>   High.
> The Holy Spirit will come upon you, and the power of the
>   Most High will overshadow you; therefore, the child to
>   be born shall be called holy, the son of God. (Luke 1:31,
>   32, 35)

In Bultmann's view, the idea of the divine origin of Jesus was not known to the disciples of Jesus; it was formed later in the Hellenistic church: "It was first added in the transformation to

Hellenism, where the idea of generation of a king or a hero from a virgin by the godhead was widespread."[2]

It seems to me that after the discovery of the Dead Sea Scrolls, the validity of Bultmann's argument should be inspected again.

One of the most exciting documents discovered in the caves at Qumran is called the "son of God" text.[3] This text speaks of a man called the "son of God and son of the Most High" and declares that he would be "great over the earth." These are exactly the terms in which the archangel Gabriel described Jesus in the annunciation to Mary just quoted.

The Qumran document (4Q246, col. 1–2) is written in Aramaic and begins with a seer's appeal to a king. The seer describes the wars that would occur in the future:[4]

Column 1

4 [. . . Through] strong [kings] oppression will come on earth.

5 [It will be war between people] and great slaughters in the provinces.

The king of Syria and Egypt is also mentioned in connection with this period of wars. After the time of wars, however, a new king would arise, and all peoples would make peace with him and serve him. This king would be called "the son of God and son of the Most High":

7 [Another/last king will arise and himself] he will be great over the earth.

8 [The kings] will do [peace with him] and all will serve [him].

9 [The son of the gre]at [Lord] he will be called, and by his
   name he shall be surnamed.[5]

1 The son of God he will be called and the son of the Most
   High they will call him.

Switching to the plural form, the document describes kings
whose reigns would "be like comets." These kings would rule the
earth for years and trample it underfoot.

1 Like comets
2 that you saw,[6] so will be their kingdom. For years they will
   rule on
3 The earth and they will trample all: People will trample on
   people and province on province.

In the passage that follows is a description of the rise of the
people of God, who would usher in an era of true peace and righteous judgment. They would be given everlasting dominion and
all states would bow down to them:

4 [vacat] [7] Until the people of God will arise and make everyone rest from the sword.
5 Its kingdom is an everlasting kingdom, and all its ways are
   in truth. It will jud[ge]
6 the earth with truth, and all will make peace. The sword
   will cease from the earth,
7 and all the provinces will pay it homage. The great God
   himself will be

Figure 11.   The "son of God" text of Qumran: 4Q246.

8   its strength. He will make war on his behalf; He will give
     nations in his hands and all of them He will cast down be-
     fore it. Its sovereignty is everlasting sovereignty.

The intriguing question prompted by this text is Who is this
figure called the "son of God" whom all peoples would make
peace with and serve, and what is his relationship to Jesus? [8]

The solution to the mysterious identity of the "son of God,"
I believe, lies in an understanding of the history of the period in
which this text was written. It is customary to date the writing
of the Qumran documents by means of paleographical testing—
that is, according to the form of a given document's script. Such
tests show that our document was written about 25 BCE.[9] But the
time the document was written is not necessarily the time it was
composed. This could be a copy of a work written earlier.[10]

I think that the apocalyptic work in this document was written in the Roman period. In my opinion, the content of the work can be clearly understood in the light of the political situation in the Roman Empire in the second half of the first century BCE.

Let us examine again the events of this period, which were already mentioned at the opening of chapter 2.

In the year 44 BCE Julius Caesar was murdered. Caesar had declared in his will that he had adopted Octavian, the son of his niece, as his son. The adopted son was now given the name of the murdered Caesar: Caesar Octavianus. In order to glorify Caesar's memory, Octavian organized games in his honor in July of 44 BCE. At the time of the games a comet appeared in the sky for seven nights in a row. This caused a great stir among the Roman populace. The comet, called *Caesaris astrum* or *sidus Iulium*, was regarded by the Romans as the soul of Caesar, which had ascended to heaven and become a god. The episode is described in Octavian's memoirs:

> On the very days of my games a comet was visible for seven
> days in the northern part of the sky. It was rising about an
> hour before sunset and was bright. . . . The common people
> believed that this star signified the soul of Caesar received
> among the spirits of the immortal gods, and on this account
> the emblem of star was added to the bust of Caesar that we
> shortly afterwards dedicated in the forum.[11]

The comet was regarded as not only a sign of Julius Caesar's divine status but also a sign of the dawning of a new era, a "golden age."[12] It was also considered an indication of the divine nature of the new ruler, Octavian.[13] Wishing to stress that he was the

Figure 12. Augustus places the star
on a statue of Julius Caesar (denarius
of L. Lentulus, Rome, 12 BCE).

son of the "divine Julius," Octavian called himself *divi filius*, which
means "son of God" or "son of the deified."[14]

The years following Caesar's murder were a time of war.
Though at first Octavian and Mark Anthony fought together
against Caesar's murderers, once the two had overcome them,
they divided the empire between them. Octavius was based in
Rome and ruled the western empire, while Mark Anthony was
based in Alexandria and ruled Egypt, Syria, and other eastern
countries. Mark Anthony's close relations with Cleopatra, queen
of Egypt, caused great tension between the two rulers, and the rivalry between them eventually resulted in the battle at Actium in
31 BCE. Anthony and Cleopatra were defeated by Octavian's fleet.
They fled to Alexandria, where they committed suicide.

Octavian was now the sole ruler of the Empire. He received
the title "Augustus"—the "exalted one"—and in many provinces
in the empire, temples and altars were set up where he was worshipped as a god. After the battle of Actium there was peace in
the empire, and a period of tranquillity and prosperity began.

I believe that the Qumran "son of God" document is connected with the events of the period, from the murder of Caesar
in 44 BCE to the decade after the battle of Actium. The beginning

of the text describes a time of wars and great distress, and it is in this context that the "king of Syria and Egypt" is mentioned. This time of troubles was the period of cruel wars between 44 and 31 BCE, and the "king of Syria and Egypt" was none other than Mark Anthony, who ruled these countries. As we have seen, the document then describes the rise of the character called the "son of God":

> [Another/last king will arise and himself] he will be great
> over the earth.
> [The kings] will do [peace with him] and all will serve [him].
> [The son of the gre]at [Lord] he will be called, and by his
> name he shall be surnamed.
> The son of God he will be called and son of the Most High
> they will call him.

Augustus—the title for Octavian—was the king who was "great on the earth" and whom all would serve. He was the sole ruler of the Roman Empire and was worshipped as a god by his subjects. Augustus was described as "son of the great Lord" because he was adopted as a son by the great ruler Julius Caesar, and he was given his name: Caesar Octavianus. The titles "son of God" and "son of the Most High" also refer to Augustus, who, as we have seen, was called *divi filius*—the son of God.

The document then says:

> Like comets
> that you saw, so will be their kingdom.

The plural form refers to the "great Lord" and his adopted son, that is, Julius Caesar and Augustus. The writer compares the reign of Caesar and Augustus to comets. A comet appeared at the time of the games organized by Augustus in Caesar's memory and became a symbol of Caesar's divinity and Augustus's rule.

The text continues:

For years they will rule on
The earth and they will trample all.

Caesar and Augustus ruled the earth for years. They trampled and oppressed the inhabitants of the empire and imposed heavy taxes upon them. The use of the word "trampled" reflects the opinion of the writer, who identified Rome as the fourth beast in Daniel's vision—of whom it was said that it would devour and trample the whole earth.[15] But the writer expected that the oppressive rule of Rome would come to an end and be replaced by the everlasting kingdom of the people of God. These people of God were for him the Danielic "son of man" (Daniel 7:13–14, 27).

Augustus represented himself as the redeemer of humanity, and many people of his generation saw him as a savior and redeemer who brought peace to the world. As we read in Suetonius, the famous writer and rhetorician Cicero dreamt of Augustus being lowered from heaven by chains of gold.[16] Jews of the period who were looking for the fulfillment of biblical prophecy could regard Augustus as the realization of the prophecy of "the son of man coming in the clouds of heaven" who would be given power and kingship and whom all peoples and tongues would worship as a god (Daniel 7:13–14).[17] The author of the Qumran document, however, disagreed with this view. In his opinion, Augustus was no more than a conqueror and oppressor. The peace of Augustus was not a genuine peace but was achieved by oppressing and trampling underfoot the peoples vanquished by the Romans. The reign of Augustus was a passing phenomenon. True peace and redemption would only come with the appearance of the real "son of man," the people of God:

> Until the people of God will arise and make everyone rest from the sword.

JESUS AS THE SON OF GOD

The three Synoptic Gospels open by introducing Jesus as the son of God. The idea of the divine origin of Jesus is found in the story of the annunciation to Joseph: "for that which is conceived in her is of the Holy Ghost" (Matthew 1:20).

Let us see again Bultmann's comments on this story:

> The idea of a divine generation from a virgin is not only foreign to the OT and to Judaism, but is completely impossible. . . . The idea of the Virgin Birth of the Messiah in particular is foreign to Judaism. . . . It was first added in the transformation to Hellenism, where the idea of the generation of a king or of a hero from a virgin by the godhead was widespread.[18]

Bultmann argues that the title "son of God" relates indeed to the idea of Jesus' divine origin, but he claims that this concept was alien to Judaism in the period of Jesus; the title "son of God" and the stories about Jesus' birth should be seen as later elements added by the Hellenistic Church after his death.

Our findings shed new light on the title "son of God." We have discovered that in the document found at Qumran, written about the year 25 BCE, that title had been applied to the Emperor Augustus. In this document, it was said of Augustus that he would be called "son of the Most High" and that he would be "great over the earth." [19] As we have seen, this corresponds exactly with the archangel Gabriel's announcement to Mary: "He will be great, and he will be called the son of the Most High. . . . Therefore, the child to be born shall be called holy, the son of God" (Luke 1 : 32, 35).

In light of the strong similarity in language between the Qumran text and the Gospel of Luke, it would seem that the description of Jesus as the son of God and the story of the annunciation did not originate, as Bultmann argued, with the Hellenistic Church. Rather, they are adaptations of materials from Qumran dating from the first century BCE. The adaptations were made by someone who was familiar with the Qumranic document and understood the Aramaic in which it was written. Hence we may conclude that the tradition of Gabriel's announcement to Mary of the divine origin of her son was formulated in the land of Israel and not within the Hellenistic Church. We can no longer rule out the possibility that Jesus indeed would have regarded himself as the "son of God."

THE MESSIAH OF QUMRAN AND ROMAN ESCHATOLOGY

The notion of the adaptation of Augustan titles to Jesus opens up the question of the possible influence of Roman and Augustan ideology on the formation of Jewish messianism in the first century BCE.

Remarkably, the figure of the Messiah and the description of the era of redemption in the messianic hymns from Qumran bear a surprising resemblance to the figure of the redeemer and the description of the "new age" in Virgil's well-known poem, the Fourth Eclogue.[20]

Virgil was a contemporary of the Qumranic Messiah. He wrote his poem in the year 40 BCE. The atmosphere in Rome in the forties of the first century BCE was one of longing for redemption. The collapse of the Republic, the civil wars, and the murder of Julius Caesar had brought a state of depression upon the Romans and a feeling that only a miraculous redeemer could save them. In the Fourth Eclogue Virgil addresses Asinius Pollio (76 BCE– 4 CE), who was consul in Rome in 40 BCE. Pollio, a well-known statesman, historian, and intellectual, was one of Virgil's patrons. Virgil assures him that in the year he served as consul a great change would occur and a new era would begin:

> And in thy consulship, Pollio, yea in thine,
> shall this glorious age begin . . .
> under thy sway,
> any lingering traces of our guilt shall become void,
> and release the earth from its continual dread.[21]

Virgil's announcement of a new age in which guilt and fear have vanished is extraordinarily similar to the proclamation of redemption in the messianic hymn from Qumran:

> Peace appears, terror ceases;
> injustice is removed],
> [and guil]t is no m[ore.[22]

In Virgil's vision the release from guilt and fear are associated with the appearance of a miraculous child. This child is the son of the gods[23] and mingles with gods and heroes:

> He shall have the gift of divine life
> shall see heroes mingled with gods and shall see himself be
> seen by them.[24]

This description recalls the words of the Qumran Messiah:

> I have taken my seat . . . in the heavens . . . I shall be reckoned
> with angels, and established in the holy congregation.[25]

In 40 BCE, the year Virgil wrote the Fourth Eclogue, Mark Anthony and Augustus reached an agreement in the city of Brindisium that led to Anthony's political marriage with Augustus's sister Octavia. The miraculous child described by Virgil appears to have been the hoped-for product of this marriage.[26] W. Clausen comments:

> To contemporary readers, the vexed question, "Who is the
> boy?" would not have occurred. They knew well enough who
> was meant: the expected son of Anthony and Octavia . . . the
> son that never was; a daughter was born instead.[27]

As we have seen, this marriage did not last. Anthony left his wife Octavia, returning to his mistress, Cleopatra, queen of Egypt. After Anthony married Cleopatra and cast Octavia out of his house, Augustus waged war against Anthony and Cleopatra. At Actium, Anthony and Cleopatra's fleet was routed by that of Augustus. Augustus now became the sole ruler of the Empire, and Virgil hailed him as the one who had realized the vision of the "son of God" and ushered in the "new age":

This, this is he, whom thou so oft hearest promised to thee,
Augustus Caesar, son of God, who shall again set up the
Golden Age.[28]

Augustus, for his part, also depicted himself as one who had
ushered in a new age.[29] He was the "son of God" who had brought
peace to the world and salvation to its inhabitants. This image of
him as redeemer of mankind is clearly reflected in this inscription of 9 BCE:

Whereas the providence which divinely ordered our lives
created . . . the most perfect good for our lives by producing
Augustus and filling him with virtue for the benefit of mankind, sending us . . . a saviour who put an end to war. . . .
When he appeared, he exceeded the hopes of all who had
anticipated good tidings. . . ."[30]

The divine character of Augustus the redeemer is also clearly
expressed in the art of the period.[31] In some artifacts Augustus is
shown sitting on a splendid throne in the company of the gods.[32]

The Messiah of the Qumran sect described himself as sitting
on a "throne of power" in the congregation of the gods,[33] exactly
as Augustus is depicted. The messianic hymns from Qumran describe the period of redemption in terms remarkably similar to
those in Virgil's description of the new age. Because the Qumranic Messiah was active during the period of Augustus, we must
consider the possibility that the political and cultural atmosphere
in Rome as expressed in Virgil's poetry and Augustus's propaganda also influenced the Messiah.

Had they heard of the Fourth Eclogue in the land of Israel?
Were the Qumran people familiar with Augustus's propa-

ganda, which represented him as a divine redeemer who ushered in a new age?

The answer to the second question has in fact already been given in the first part of this appendix. We have seen that the Qumran "son of God" text touches on certain cardinal points of Augustus's ideology: the description of Augustus as the "son of God" and mention of the comet that augured a new era.

It now appears that we can also give a positive answer to the first question.

The Fourth Eclogue, as we have seen, was addressed to Asinius Pollio, who was consul in 40 BCE and a patron of Virgil. We now find that Herod had a special relationship with Asinius Pollio. They first became acquainted in 40 BCE, the year in which the Fourth Eclogue was written. At that time, Mattathias Antigonus, the last of the Hasmonean rulers, had taken office in Judea with the help of the Parthians. Herod fled from Antigonus and his Parthian supporters and reached Rome, where he turned to Mark Anthony for his help. On Anthony's initiative and with the agreement of Augustus, the Roman Senate came to assembly and proclaimed Herod the king of Judea. After the Senate had dispersed, Anthony and Augustus made their way to the Capitol, with Herod between them. The procession was headed by the consuls in office that year: Caius Domitius Calvinus and Asinius Pollio.[34]

The connection between Pollio and Herod grew stronger in the following years. In 22 BCE, Herod sent his sons Alexander and Aristobulus to Rome for their education. The boys stayed in Rome for about five years and lived in the home of Pollio, whom Josephus described as having a special relationship with Herod.[35] It can therefore be assumed that Herod and his court were indeed aware of the Fourth Eclogue, which Virgil had addressed to Pollio.

In view of all this, I claim that it is possible that the Messiah of Qumran was influenced by the Roman vision of redemption and Augustus's propaganda. Augustus was depicted as a ruler with a divine nature, fusing the earth with the kingdom of heaven. It is in this spirit that the Qumranic Messiah describes his relationship with God and his position in heaven in terms derived from a royal court. He depicts himself as "the king's friend"—i.e., the friend of God—and describes himself as equal to the "king's sons," the angels. In the messianic hymn from Qumran we find a picture without precedent in Jewish literature: the portrait of a Messiah with a divine nature sitting on a lofty throne in heaven and associating with the angels. This Messiah ushers in a new age in which guilt, sin, and fear have disappeared. It is possible that this portrait was fashioned under the influence of Virgil's message of redemption and release from guilt, and the artistic depictions of Augustus sitting on a throne surrounded by gods.[36]

ABBREVIATIONS

ANRW	*Aufsteig und Niedergang der Romischen Welt*
BBR	*Buletinul Bibliotecii Romane*
BICS	*Bulletin of the Institute of Classical Studies*, University of London
CBQMS	*Catholic Biblical Quarterly, Monograph Series*
CQ	E. Qimron, ed., "The Text of CDC," in *The Damascus Document Reconsidered*, ed. M. Broshi, Jerusalem 1992, pp. 9–49
CR	*Classical Review*
DJD	*Discoveries in the Judean Desert*, Oxford 1955–
DSD	*Dead Sea Discoveries*
Ebib	Études Biblique
HTR	*Harvard Theological Review*
ICC	*International Critical Commentary*

JBL	*Journal of Biblical Literature*
JQR	*Jewish Quarterly Review*
JRS	*Journal of Roman Studies*
JSOT	*Journal for the Study of the Old Testament*
JSQ	*Jewish Studies Quarterly*
JTS	*Journal of Theological Studies*
NT	*Novum Testamentum*
NTS	*New Testament Studies*
RBPH	*Revue Belge de Philologie et d'Histoire*
RQ	*Revue de Qumran*
TAPA	*Transactions and Proceedings of the American Philological Association*
TDNT	*Theological Dictionary of the New Testament* 1–9, Grand Rapids 1964–74
TDOT	*Theological Dictionary of the Old Testament* 1–, Grand Rapids 1974–
ZDPV	*Zeitschrift des Deutschen Palästina-Vereins*

NOTES

PREFACE

1. R. A. Kugler, "Holiness, Purity, the Body, and Society," JSOT 76 (1997), p. 5.

INTRODUCTION

1. At the most, he confirmed his messiahship in response to the statements of others. See Matthew 16:17, 22:64; Mark 14:62; Luke 22:70.

2. Matthew 16:20; Mark 8:30; Luke 4:35, 9:21.

3. Matthew 16:21, 17:12, 20:18–19; Mark 8:31, 9:12, 31, 10:33–34, 14:21; Luke 9:22, 44, 18:31–33.

4. For a survey of the literature on this question, see J. C. O'Neill, *Who Did Jesus Think He Was?* (Leiden, 1995), p. 7ff.

5. W. Wrede, *Das Messiasgeheimnis in den Evangelien* (Göttingen, 1901); R. Bultmann, *Theology of the New Testament*, trans. K. Groebel (New York, 1951) (originally published as *Theologie des Neuen Testament* [Tübingen 1948]), p. 26ff.

6. Bultmann, *Theology of the New Testament*, p. 31. See also Vermes's words: "Neither the suffering of the Messiah, nor his death and resurrection appear to have been part of the faith of first-century Judaism." G. Vermes, *Jesus the Jew* (Philadelphia, 1981), p. 38.

7. Wrede, *Das Messiasgeheimnis*, pp. 82–92; Bultmann, *Theology of the New Testament*, p. 31; idem, *The History of the Synoptic Tradition* (Oxford, 1963), p. 152.

8. See, however, the criticism of Bultmann's method and the new approach of Helmut Koester in his very important study "The Memory of Jesus' Death and the Worship of the Risen Lord," *HTR* 91 (1998), pp. 334–50 and note 23.

CHAPTER 1. THE MESSIANIC SECRET

1. The palace stood in the area to the south of today's Jaffa Gate.

2. The Essenes were a Jewish sect. Most scholars think that they wrote the scrolls found at Qumran known as the Dead Sea Scrolls. The Essene Quarter was in the area known today as Mount Zion. We know this neighborhood was there from the location of the Essene Gate, the remains of which have been discovered on the southern slopes of Mount Zion. An archaeological excavation on the site revealed that the gate was inserted in the city wall during the reign of King Herod. See B. Pixner, D. Chen, and Sh. Margalit, "Mount Zion: 'The Gate of the Essenes Reexcavated,'" *ZDPV* 105 (1989), pp. 85–95. On the Essene Quarter on Mount Zion, see R. Raisner, "Jesus, the Primitive Community, and the Essene Quarter of Jerusalem," in *Jesus and the Dead Sea Scrolls*, ed. J. H. Charlesworth (New York, 1992). We also know about the Essene residences in Jerusalem at that period from the remains of an Essene cemetery discovered by B. Zissu. See B. Zissu, "'Qumran Type' Graves in Jerusalem: Archeological Evidence of an Essene Community?" *DSD* 5 (1988) pp. 158–71.

3. See Josephus, *Jewish War* 2.128, Loeb Classical Library (Cambridge, Mass., 1928).

4. See J. M. Baumgarten, "Qumran Cave 4 XIII," *DJD* 18 (Oxford, 1996), p. 181; and A. Steudel, "The Houses of Prostration," *RQ* 16 (1993–95), pp. 49–66.

5. On the Essene morning prayers, see Josephus, *Jewish War* 2.128. On morning prayers in the Dead Sea literature, see M. Weinfeld, "The Morning Prayers in Qumran and in Conventional Jewish Literature," in *Memorial Jean Carmignac*, ed. E. Puech and F. Garcia Martinez (Paris, 1988), pp. 481–94; idem, "On the Question of Morning Benedictions at Qumran," *Tarbiz* 51 (1982), pp. 495–96; R. Brody, "Morning Benedictions at Qumran?" *Tarbiz* 51 (1982), pp. 493–94; and D. Falk, *Daily, Sabbath, and Festival Prayers in the Dead Sea Scrolls* (Leiden, 1998), pp. 21–124.

6. See Josephus, *Jewish Antiquities* 15.317, Loeb Classical Library (Cambridge, Mass., 1930).

7. Josephus, *Jewish War* 1.401.

8. Ibid., 5.172–83.

9. On the dovecotes, see ibid.; on Herod's doves, see Mishna, Hulin 12:1.

10. See Josephus, *Jewish Antiquities* 15.228; idem, *Jewish War* 1.538, 571, 620. On Herod's courts of law, see A. M. Rabello, "*Hausgericht* in the House of Herod the Great?" (Hebrew) in *Jerusalem in the Second Temple Period: A. Shalit Memorial Volume*, ed. A. Oppenheimer, U. Rappaport, and M. Stern (Jerusalem, 1980), pp. 119–35.

11. 4Q525, col. 4:23–5; E. Puech, "Qumran Grotte 4," *DJD* 25 (Oxford, 1998), p. 146.

12. As Herod's palace has not survived, we cannot know the exact nature of the wall paintings it contained. Here I have based my description on the wall paintings discovered in Herod's palace in Massada. In these paintings there are geometrical designs that bear a remarkable resemblance to those found in Augustus's palace. See J. Geiger, "Herod and Rome: New Aspects," in *The Jews in the Hellenistic-Roman World: Studies in Memory of Menahem Stern*, ed. I. M. Gafni, A. Oppenheimer, and D. R. Schwartz (Jerusalem, 1996), p. 139 (Hebrew).

13. In describing the meal I have followed Geiger, "Herod and Rome," p. 145. The description is based mainly on the discoveries at Massada. On the fish sauce sent to Herod from Rome, see H. M. Cotton and J. Geiger, *Massada II: The Yigael Yadin Excavations 1963–65. Final Reports. The Latin and Greek Documents* (Jerusalem, 1989), pp. 166–67.

14. See Cotton and Geiger, *Massada II*, pp. 163–64.

15. Concerning this consignment of wine, see ibid., pp. 140–49. Cotton and Geiger assume that the wine must have been sent to Herod sometime between the month of January and the twelfth of October in 19 BCE. The journey by sea from Italy to Jerusalem took between 55 and 73 days (see H. W. Hoehner, *Herod Antipas* [Grand Rapids, 1980], p. 35). Even if the consignment left Italy at the beginning of October of 19 BCE, it may be assumed that the wine had reached Jerusalem by January of 18 BCE.

16. On stone utensils in Jerusalem, see N. Avigad, *The Upper City of Jerusalem* (Jerusalem, 1980), pp. 174–76 (Hebrew).

17. See M. Stern, *Studies in Jewish History: The Second Temple Period* (Jerusalem, 1991), pp. 445–64 (Hebrew).

18. Josephus, *Jewish Antiquities* 15.343. Josephus says that their host was "Pollio." On the identification of this "Pollio" with Asinius Pollio, see L. H. Feldman, "Asinius Pollio and His Jewish Interests," *TAPA* 84 (1953), pp. 73–80; idem, "Asinius Pollio and Herod's Sons," *CQ* 35 (1985), pp. 240–43; Stern, *Studies in Jewish History*, p. 175.

19. See Taylor, *The Divinity of the Roman Emperor* (Middletown, 1931), p. 174.

20. See Reisner, "Jesus, the Primitive Community, and the Essene Quarter," p. 213.

21. See Josephus, *Jewish War* 2.123.

22. See 1QSa 2:11–17.

23. Josephus, *Jewish War* 2.130.

24. Ibid., 2.131; 1QSa 2:18–21.

25. Josephus, *Jewish War* 2.130.

26. Ibid., 2.131. See also M. Weinfeld, "Grace after Meals at the

Mourner's House in a Text from Qumran," *Tarbiz* 61 (1991), pp. 15–24 (Hebrew).

27. On the blessing of the *nasi*, see O. P. Barthelemy and J. T. Milik, "1QSa 20–28," *DJD* 1 (Oxford, 1955), pp. 127–28.

28. See Isaiah 11:4.

29. "People of Kittim" was the term commonly used for the Romans in the Dead Sea writings. On the expectation that the king of Kittim would be slain by the *nasi* of the community, see D. Flusser, "The Death of the Evil King," in *A Light for Jacob: Studies in the Bible and the Dead Sea Scrolls in Memory of J. S. Licht*, ed. Y. Hoffman and J. H. Pollak (Jerusalem, 1997), pp. 254–62 (Hebrew).

30. See Josephus, *Jewish Antiquities* 15.366.

31. Josephus, *Jewish War* 2.141.

32. See 1QM 15:2.

33. See the reconstruction by M. Broshi, which I have partly followed: "A Day in the Life of Hananiah Nothos: A Story," in *A Day in Qumran*, ed. A. Roitman (Jerusalem, 1997), pp. 61–70.

34. E. L. Sukenik, *Otzar ha-Megiloth ha-genuzoth* (Jerusalem, 1954), pp. 21, 32.

35. For a detailed discussion of the different manuscripts, see appendix A.

36. E. Schuller, "A Hymn from a Cave Four Hodayot Manuscript," *JBL* 112 (1993), pp. 605–28.

37. See the Thanksgivings Scroll 40:30–31, 12:24–29. On the marked contrast between the sense of guilt prevailing in the thanksgiving psalms and the feeling of release from guilt in these hymns, see J. J. Collins, *The Scepter and the Star* (New York, 1995), p. 148.

38. "כלה עוון": see Schuller, "A Hymn," p. 609, lines 6–7.

39. Ibid., pp. 627–28; J. J. Collins, *Apocalypticism in the Dead Sea Scrolls* (London and New York, 1997), p. 147.

40. The reconstruction proposed here is, generally speaking, based on that in E. Eshel, "The Identification of the 'Speaker' of the Self-Glorification Hymn," in *The Provo International Conference on the Dead*

Sea Scrolls, ed. D. W. Parry and E. Ulrich (Leiden, 1999), pp. 619–35; and idem, "471b: 4Q Self-Glorification Hymn," *DJD* 29 (Oxford, 1999), pp. 427–28. I have deviated from her reconstruction in a few places, which I shall indicate in the notes to the detailed discussion of the text in appendix A.

41. The use of the term אלים, *elim*, for the angels is very common in the Dead Sea literature.

42. Compare "the king's friend," 1 Chronicles 27:33.

43. On "holy ones" as a term for angels, see Psalm 89:6–8. As a matter of fact, I believe that the title ידיד המלך, "the king's friend," has a double meaning here and includes also a reference to the earthly king Herod. This will be discussed in length in chapter 3.

44. 4Q491 frg. 11, col. 1:5–6. I follow Eshel's translation (Eshel, "The 'Speaker,'" p. 622). For a full translation of the hymn, see appendix A.

45. The first sentence appears in line 10 and the second sentence in lines 9–10 of 4Q491 frg. 11, col. 1. Here I have reversed the order.

46. Ibid., line 10.

47. For a detailed examination of the scholarship on the subject, see appendix A.

48. J. J. Collins, *Apocalypticism in the Dead Sea Scrolls*, London and New York, 1997, p. 147.

49. The possibility that the figure in question was a messianic leader was briefly considered, among other possibilities, in E. Puech, "La croyance des Esséniens en la vie future: Immortalité, résurrection, vie éternelle?" *Ebib* 22 (Paris, 1993), pp. 392–95.

50. See Eshel, "The 'Speaker,'" pp. 620–21.

51. See notes 36 and 37, this chapter.

52. 4Q427 frg. 7, col. 2:8–9. The translation is according to 4Q427 frg. 7 in E. Schuller's edition (see Schuller, "A Hymn").

53. See 1QHa 11:22–27. See the detailed discussion in appendix A.

54. The translation given here is based on a combination of text CD

14:18–19 and the fragment from cave four. See J. M. Baumgarten, "Messianic Forgiveness of Sin in CD 14:19 (4Q266 frg. 10, col. 1:12–13)," in *The Provo International Conference on the Dead Sea Scrolls*, ed. D. W. Perry and E. Ulrich (Leiden, 1999), pp. 537–44.

55. 4Q491 frg. 11, col. 1; Eshel ("The 'Speaker,'" p. 622, line 15) translates "of the Mess[iah]." However, my translation is more precise.

56. 4Q491 frg. 11, col. 1:15. In the manuscript, the formulation is [ ]קרן מש. The last letter could be ש or ע. The reconstruction [מש]יח was proposed by D. Dimant in "A Synoptic Comparison of Parallel Sections in 4Q427 7, 4Q491 11 and 4Q471b," *JQR* 85 (1994), p. 159.

57. See the detailed discussion of the subject in appendix A.

58. This is a combination of the two versions of the first hymn.

59. See Baumgarten, "Messianic Forgiveness of Sin."

60. For a survey of the literature concerning the "historical Jesus," see B. Chilton and C. A. Evans, eds., *Studying the Historical Jesus* (Leiden, 1994).

61. Wrede, *Das Messiasgeheimnis*; Bultmann, *Theology of the New Testament*, vol. 1, p. 26ff.

62. Daniel 7:9–14.

63. Bultmann, *Theology of the New Testament*, vol. 1, p. 31.

64. This claim of superiority to the angels, "Who is like me among the angels?" (4QHe frg. 1:4) is unknown elsewhere in Qumran literature. It is dramatically different from the regular formula about communion with the angels in these writings (see 1QHa 3:22 and elsewhere).

65. See 4Q491 frg. 11, col. 1:5–6.

66. On the superiority over the angels, see Psalm 89:7.

67. 4Q491 frg. 11, col. 1:9.

68. Version 1 of the hymns exists in three manuscripts: 4QHa, 4QHe, and 1QHa. Manuscript 4QHa is dated by Schuller (in her edition: "431: 4Q Hodayot," *DJD* 29 [Oxford, 1999], p. 202) to the early Herodian period. (The term "early Herodian period" in paleographic scholarship refers to the second half of the first century BCE, a period

that roughly corresponds to the reign of King Herod: 37–34 BCE.) F. M. Cross has dated 4QHa to about 25 BCE. (See note 14 in Schuller's edition: "427: 4Q Hodayot," *DJD* 29 [Oxford, 1999], p. 85.)

The third manuscript is the copy of the Thanksgivings Scroll from cave 1 in Qumran, 1QHa, containing fragments of the hymns. This copy is dated by F. M. Cross to between 30 and 1 BCE. See F. M. Cross, "The Development of the Jewish Script," in *The Bible and the Ancient Near East: Essays in Honor of W. F. Allbright*, ed. G. W. Wright (Garden City, 1961), p. 137.

Version 2 of the hymns exists in only one manuscript: 4Q491 11. This manuscript has been dated to the second half of the first century BCE. See *DJD* 7, ed. M. Baillet (Oxford, 1982), p. 12; M. G. Abegg, "Who Ascended to Heaven? 4Q491, 4Q427, and the Teacher of Righteousness," in *Eschatology, Messianism, and the Dead Sea Scrolls*, ed. C. A. Evans and P. W. Flint (Grand Rapids, 1997), p. 65.

69. Herod ruled between the years 37–4 BCE.

CHAPTER 2. AFTER THREE DAYS

1. See Taylor, *Divinity of the Roman Emperor*, p. 106; and D. Fishwick, *The Imperial Cult in the Latin West* (Leiden, 1987), vol. 1, p. 76. Octavian began to use this title around the year 40 BCE.

2. At first there was the Second Triumvirate, which also included Lapidus, but after a time he was driven out by Octavian.

3. Plutarch, "Anthony," in *The Lives of the Noble Grecians and Romans*, trans. J. Dryden (Chicago, 1952).

4. Justin Martyr, 1 Apology 44, ed. P. Marani (Paris, 1857).

5. See Clemens Alexandrinus, *Strom.* 6.5.30, ed. N. le Nowry (Paris, 1890). See E. Schürer, *The History of the Jewish People in the Age of Jesus Christ*, rev. and ed. G. Vermes, F. Millar, and M. Goodman (London, 1995), vol. 3, part 1, p. 655.

6. D. Flusser, *Judaism and the Origins of Christianity* (Jerusalem, 1988), pp. 392–448. As was noted by Hinnells, the Oracle contains gen-

uine Persian elements (J. R. Hinnells, "The Zoroastrian Doctrine of Salvation in the Roman World," in *Man and His Salvation: Studies in Memory of S. G. F. Brandon*, ed. E. J. Sharp and J. R. Hinnells [Manchester, 1973], pp. 125–48). It is possible that the Jewish author indeed used a Persian apocalypse (see Flusser). However, he blended the Persian elements with biblical ones.

7. Lactantius, *Divin. Inst.* 7.16.4, ed. S. Brandt (New York, 1965). Flusser's translation in Flusser, *Judaism*, p. 402 ff.

8. Hystaspes said that the second king would come from Syria. For an explanation of this, see notes 48 and 52, this chapter. He said that the first king would come from the north. Flusser (*Judaism*, pp. 65–67) explains that this is an attempt to create an association with the "king of the north" in chapter 11 of the Book of Daniel. There are other elements adopted from the Book of Daniel in the description of the first king. Compare: ". . . having destroyed three of that number (of kings)" (Lactantius, *Divin. Inst.* 7.16.3)—"and shall put down three kings" (Daniel 7:24); ". . . he will change the laws" (Lactantius, *Divin. Inst.* 7.16.4)—". . . and shall think to change the time and the laws" (Daniel 7:25).

9. Lactantius, *Divin. Inst.* 7.17. 4.

10. See the description of these events in R. Syme, *The Roman Revolution* (Oxford, 1939), pp. 259–93.

11. Dio Cassius, *Roman History* 50.4.1, Loeb Classical Library (Cambridge, Mass., 1917).

12. The attempt to make Alexandria the new Rome is reflected in the coins of that period. See Taylor, *Divinity of the Roman Emperor*, p. 127 and note 55.

13. Lactantius, *Divin. Inst.* 7.17.4–5.

14. The connection was made by D. Flusser (*Judaism*, p. 433 ff.).

15. See the survey of recent scholarship and discussion of the subject in Thomas B. Slater, "On the Social Setting of the Revelation of John," *New Testament Studies* 44 (1998), pp. 232–56.

16. In the original text it may have been a goat's horns, and John, the

author of the book, may have changed the goat into a lamb in order to point to the contrast between Jesus, described as a lamb, and the Antichrist, who looks like a lamb but speaks like a dragon. See J. Jeremias, *TDNT* 1:341.

17. Suetonius, "Augustus," 94, in *The Lives of the Caesars*, trans. J. C. Rolfe (London, 1913). Suetonius is not consistent here, as in section 5 he says that Augustus was born in September. The Capricorn was the sign of his conception and not of his birth. See G. W. Bowersock, "The Pontificate of Augustus," in *Between Republic and Empire*, ed. A. Raaflaub and M. Toher (Berkeley, 1990), p. 386.

18. J. R. Fears, *The Divine Election of the Emperor as a Political Concept at Rome* (Rome, 1977), pp. 207–10. For a detailed discussion of the various implications of Augustus's use of the sign of the Capricorn, see T. S. Barton, *Power and Knowledge* (Ann Arbor, 1994), pp. 40–44.

19. J. Gage, *Apollon romain* (Paris, 1955), pp. 583–637; E. Simon, *Die Portlandvase* (Mainz, 1957), p. 30ff.

20. Dio Cassius, *Roman History* 45.1.2.

21. Suetonius, "Augustus," 94.

22. On Apollo's struggle with the Python, see J. Fontenrose, *Python: A Study of Delphic Myth and Its Origins* (Berkeley, 1959).

23. See S. Weinstock, *Divus Julius* (Oxford, 1971), p. 14.

24. Propertius, *Elegies* 4.6.27, Loeb Classical Library (Cambridge, Mass., 1990).

25. On the temple of Apollo and Augustus, see K. Galinski, *Augustan Culture* (Princeton, 1996), pp. 213–24.

26. Taylor, *Divinity of the Roman Emperor*, p. 154 and note 27.

27. Fishwick, *Development of the Imperial Cult*, vol. 1, p. 81, note 70.

28. Suetonius, "Augustus," 96–97.

29. On the prophetic powers ascribed to the Python, see Fontenrose, *Python*, p. 374. Fontenrose (p. 375ff.) speaks of the close connection between the Python and Dionysius. As we know, Mark Anthony saw himself as Dionysius. Perhaps the author of the vision wished to

turn the myth of Augustus on its head here. Augustus compared himself to Apollo, who defeated the Python-Dionysius, but in fact, says the author, he himself was a dragon, like the Python-Dionysius!

30. A. Yarbro Collins, in *The Combat Myth in the Book of Revelation* (Harvard Dissertations in Religion [Missoula, 1976], p. 64ff.), saw that the episode in chapter 12 of the Book of Revelation about the dragon that persecuted the woman who bore the Messiah was based on the myth of the Python, who persecuted Leto, the mother of Apollo. In her opinion (p. 128), the author of the vision was a Jew who wrote this work in Asia Minor in the first century CE. This story, she claimed (pp. 188–89), reflected a polemic against the propaganda disseminated by Augustus and the Caesars who followed him. The author of the vision asserts that the Roman Caesar was not Apollo, as he boastfully claimed, but the dragon Python; the true Apollo is the Jewish Messiah. Collins's suggestions are convincing. It would seem that the story of the persecution of the mother of the Messiah by the dragon and the vision of the two beasts in chapter 13 of Revelation originated with the same writer. This writer was familiar with the mythology concerning the god Apollo and with the stories connected with the temple at Delphi. He exploited this knowledge in order to assail Augustus's propaganda. Concerning the period in which he was writing, see note 46, this chapter. John, the writer of the Book of Revelation, included the vision of the two beasts in chapter 13 of his book, making various additions to the original vision. Among these additions one must include the reference to Jesus in verse 8 and the hints of the forced imposition of the Caesar cult in verses 9 and 15. If the "number of the beast" in verse 18 refers to Nero, this verse is also one of John's additions.

31. R. H. Charles, "The Revelation of St. John," *ICC* (Edinburgh, 1994), pp. 345–46; W. J. Harrington, "Revelation," *Sacra Pagina* 16 (Collegeville, 1993), p. 140.

32. See the references in Charles, "Revelation of St. John," p. 349. Charles disagrees with this interpretation, saying that according to

verse 3, the mortal wound only affected one of the heads and not the entire beast, but this claim is not decisive. In verses 12 and 14 it is specifically said that the wound endangered the beast's very existence.

33. Suetonius, "Augustus," 52. See also G. W. Bowersock, *Augustus and the Greek World* (Oxford, 1965), p. 116.

34. Writings of this kind apparently also existed among Greeks who opposed Augustus's rule. See Bowersock, *Augustus and the Greek World*, p. 110.

35. On the imperial cult in Asia Minor, see S. F. R. Price, *Rituals and Power: The Roman Imperial Cult in Asia Minor* (Cambridge, 1984).

36. Lactantius, *Divin. Inst.* 7.17.1–2.

37. Ibid., 7.17.3

38. Revelation 11:3–6.

39. It seems that the Oracle of Hystaspes combined the two into a single figure, the "prophet of God," in order to heighten the contrast between the false prophet and the prophet of God. For that reason the messianic aspect was also left out. In this way the confrontation between the two prophets was given greater emphasis. Flusser (*Judaism*, p. 421) thought the formulation in Hystaspes was the original one and that John split the figure of the prophet into two. But, in my opinion, the use of the Book of Zechariah and the oblique comparisons to Moses and Elijah show that there was an authentic tradition of two Messiahs—a royal Messiah and a priestly Messiah. The Church Fathers, who saw these as typological figures, identified the two witnesses as Elijah and Enoch, who went up to heaven. As we shall see, the story in chapter 11 of the Book of Revelation is solidly grounded in the historical events of the year 4 BCE, and therefore the two witnesses also have to be identified as historical figures.

40. See W. H. Brownlee, "John the Baptist in the New Light of Ancient Scrolls," in *The New Scrolls and the New Testament*, ed. K. Stendahl (New York, 1957), p. 47.

41. In the Greek original, the term used for witnesses is *martyr*. On

the history of the term *martyr*, see G. W. Bowersock, *Martyrdom and Rome* (Cambridge, 1995), pp. 5–21.

42. The word *abyssos* has various meanings (on the different meanings of this word, see J. Massyngberde-Ford, "Revelation," *Anchor Bible* [Garden City, 1975], p. 152). It can refer to the depths of the sea and also the depths of the earth. If we interpret it as referring here to the depths of the earth, we would have to identify the beast ascending from these depths as the second beast in chapter 13 of Revelation, which is described as coming up from the earth (see Flusser, *Judaism*, p. 449, note 192). That is to say, it is the beast that is also described as a false prophet and so resembles Augustus. But if we interpret the word as referring to the depths of the sea, we would have to identify the beast ascending from the abyss as the first beast in chapter 13, which comes up from the sea (see A. Y. Collins, *Combat Myth*, p. 165). Of this beast it is said that "it was allowed to make war on the saints and to conquer them" (13:7). This recalls the statement in chapter 11 of Revelation about the beast that ascends from the abyss: "The beast that ascends from the abyss will make war upon them and conquer them and kill them." We have already identified the beast coming from the sea as the Roman Empire, which had recovered from the murder of Julius Caesar. Hence both these possibilities lead to the same conclusion: the two witnesses were killed by the Roman imperial army, the army of Augustus. This agrees with Hystaspes' version, according to which the "son of God"—Augustus—killed the prophet of God.

43. The words "where also our Lord was crucified" in chapter 11, verse 8, were an addition by John to the Jewish source he was using.

44. Josephus, *Jewish Antiquities* 17.213–18; idem, *Jewish War* 3.1.2. The revolt appears to have been crushed in August. See Hoehner, *Herod Antipas*, p. 37. The revolt lasted for about five months. This may have been the background for the reference to a period of five months in Revelation 9:5.

45. Josephus, *Jewish Antiquities* 17.261–62; idem, *Jewish War* 2.3.3.

This is the background to Hystaspes' assertion (Lactantius, *Divin. Inst.* 7.17.6) that the wicked king—the "false prophet"—would try to destroy the Temple.

46. J. Wellhausen thought that these verses expressed the views of the Zealots in the great rebellion against Rome. But in the great rebellion the outer court, the altar, and the Temple were all captured (Josephus, *Jewish War* 6.4.6), so the description in the Book of Revelation does not correspond to the historical reality of 70 CE. On the other hand, the events of 4 BCE are perfectly in accord with what is written in the Book of Revelation. As Charles and other scholars have thought, John, the author of the Book of Revelation, drew on an early Jewish source. As I have pointed out (note 28, this chapter), the vision of the persecution of the Messiah's mother in chapter 12 and the vision of the two beasts in chapter 13 and in verses 1–13 of chapter 11 also, in my opinion, derive from this source. It is possible that the passages were written by someone whose native language was Hebrew or Aramaic—an idea supported by the large number of Semitic linguistic forms that appear in these sections of the Book of Revelation. See S. Thompson, *The Apocalypse and Semitic Syntax* (Cambridge, 1985), p. 107 (on chapters 11 and 12). Because the events of the revolt of 4 BCE are reflected here, one can say with certainty that the work was written after that date, and it seems that the time of writing was the beginning of the first century CE. As I have said (note 30, this chapter), A. Yarbro Collins thinks that the Jewish author of the vision of the persecution of the Messiah's mother was writing in Asia Minor. I tend to agree with this view. Perhaps the author was a Jew who fled from the land of Israel when the revolt was put down and settled in Asia Minor. There he became acquainted with the various legends connected with Apollo that were current in that area (see Collins, *Combat Myth*, pp. 245–52) and made use of them in his criticism of Augustus. A similar case of a Jew who fled from the land of Israel at the time of the crushing of a revolt against the Romans and settled in Asia Minor is that of Trypho, known for his debate with Justin Martyr. Trypho left

the land of Israel during the crushing of the Bar-Kochba rebellion and settled in Ephesus.

The idea that John, the author of the Book of Revelation, used Jewish sources in his book has been raised many times in scholarly literature: see D. E. Aune, "Revelation 1–5," *Word Biblical Commentary* (Dallas, 1997), cx–cxvii. From John's point of view, this material was in keeping with his criticism of the imperial cult and his conception of freedom. See E. Schuessler-Fiorenza, *The Book of Revelation, Justice, and Judgment* (Philadelphia, 1985), pp. 35–84.

47. In rabbinical chronography, the revolt was named after Quintilius Varus. See Ch. J. Milikowski, "Seder Olam, a Rabbinic Chronography" (Ph.D. diss., Yale University, 1981), p. 441. On Quintilius Varus, see R. Syme, *Augustan Aristocracy* (Oxford, 1986), pp. 313ff.

48. This is the background to Hystaspes' description of the wicked king as someone coming from Syria (see note 8, this chapter). His description of Augustus as coming to the land of Israel from Syria represents a fusion of the figure of Augustus with that of Varus, his governor in Syria. A similar phenomenon can be seen in the description of these events in *The Assumption of Moses* 6.8–9 (see R. H. Charles, *Apocrypha and Pseudepigrapha of the Old Testament in English* [Oxford, 1913], vol. 2, p. 419). See also note 52, this chapter.

49. See Josephus, *Jewish Antiquities* 17.291–92; idem, *Against Apion* 1.7, Loeb Classical Library (Cambridge, Mass., 1926).

50. Josephus, *Jewish Antiquities* 17.289, 295; idem, *Jewish War* 2.5.1–2.

51. *The Assumption of Moses* 6.8–9.

52. Here, as in the Oracle of Hystaspes (see note 48, this chapter), there is a fusion of the figures of Augustus and Varus. In *The Assumption of Moses* the actions of Varus are ascribed to Augustus, king of the west, and in Hystaspes the actions of Varus are ascribed to Augustus, who is described as coming from Syria.

53. 1QM 19:11. See Flusser, *Judaism*, p. 430.

54. On the two Messiahs in the Qumran literature, see D. Goodblatt, *The Monarchic Principle* (Tübingen, 1994), pp. 65–71; J. J. Collins, *Scepter and the Star*, pp. 74–101; M. Abegg, "The Messiah at Qumran: Are We Still Seeing Double?" *DSD* 2 (1995), pp. 125–44; J. VanderKam, "Messianism in the Scrolls," in *The Community of the Renewed Covenant: The Notre Dame Symposium on the Dead Sea Scrolls*, ed. E. Ulrich and J. VanderKam (Notre Dame, 1994), pp. 212–34; F. M. Cross, "Notes on the Doctrine of the Two Messiahs at Qumran," in *Current Research and Technological Developments on the Dead Sea Scrolls*, ed. D. W. Parry and S. D. Ricks (Leiden, 1996), pp. 1–4; W. M. Schniedewind, "Structural Aspects of Qumran Messianism in the Damascus Document," in *The Provo International Conference on the Dead Sea Scrolls*, ed. D. W. Parry and E. Ulrich (Leiden, 1999), pp. 523–36.

55. See Eshel, "The 'Speaker,'" p. 622, line 5; p. 620, line 9.

56. For parallel cases of denial of burial for three days, see S. Lieberman, *Texts and Studies* (New York, 1974), p. 258.

57. G. Scholem, *The Messianic Idea in Judaism* (New York, 1971), pp. 87–88.

58. See appendix A.

59. See also "He shall wear out the saints of the Most High" (Daniel 7:25) and "He shall destroy mighty men and the people of the saints" (Daniel 8:24).

60. "The beast that ascends from the bottomless pit will make war upon them and conquer them and kill them" (Revelation 11:7) and "He shall fight against the prophet of God and shall overcome" (Lactantius, *Divin. Inst.* 7.17:3). See also Flusser, *Judaism*, p. 62, note 170.

61. One could also find confirmation of the killing of the Messiah in Daniel: "The anointed one shall be cut off and shall have nothing, and the city and the sanctuary shall be destroyed" (9:26). Jerome, in his commentary on Daniel, said that the Jews interpreted this verse as referring to the Messiah. As this interpretation is not found in any of the known Jewish commentaries, it is possible that it originated with the disciples of the Messiah of Qumran.

62. In the Masoretic text it is written: "They shall look on me whom they have pierced." The version "They shall look on him whom they have pierced" is found in the translations of Aquila, Symmachos, and Theodotion.

63. "Men from the peoples and tribes and tongues and nations will gaze at their dead bodies" (Revelation 9:11). Another motif is the sight of the Messiahs ascending to heaven: "And in the sight of their foes they went up to heaven in a cloud" (Revelation 11:12). A similar description is found in Hystaspes: "And while all look on and wonder" (Lactantius 7.17.3).

64. See Scholem, *Messianic Idea*, pp. 8–18.

65. Daniel 7:9–13.

66. See Revelation 11:12; Lactantius 7.17.3.

67. See the description of the descent of the redeemer from the heavens and the eschatological war in Hystaspes, quoted in Lactantius 7.19.2–8. Christian motifs have been added but, as Flusser saw (*Judaism*, pp. 406–42), one can clearly recognize the original motifs of Hystaspes' description. These motifs have interesting parallels in the Qumran literature and in midrashic literature.

68. This date is based on the story of the "massacre of the innocents" in Matthew, chapter 2, from which we may deduce that Herod was still alive when Jesus was about two years old. As we have seen, Herod died in 4 BCE. For a discussion of the various estimates of Jesus' date of birth, see G. Ogg, "The Age of Jesus When He Taught," *NTS* 5 (1958–59), pp. 291–98; J. P. Meier, *A Marginal Jew* (New York, 1987), vol. 1, pp. 375–78.

69. For a discussion of Jesus' relationship with the Judaism of his time, see E. P. Sanders, *Jesus and Judaism* (Philadelphia, 1985); H. Falk, *Jesus the Pharisee: A New Look at the Jewishness of Jesus* (New York, 1985); J. H. Charlesworth, ed., *Jesus's Jewishness, Exploring the Place of Jesus within Early Judaism* (New York, 1990); Vermes, *Jesus the Jew*.

70. Vermes, *Jesus the Jew*, p. 58ff.; D. Flusser, *Jesus* (Jerusalem, 1997), p. 113; S. Safrai, "Jesus and the Hassidic Movement," in *The Jews*

in the Hellenistic-Roman World: Studies in Memory of Menahem Stern, ed. I. M. Gafni, A. Oppenheimer, and D. R. Schwartz (Jerusalem, 1996), pp. 413–36.

71. Vermes, *Jesus the Jew*, pp. 77–78; Flusser, *Judaism*, pp. 469–89.

72. On Jesus' parables in relation to those of the Sages, see the studies listed in D. Stern, *Parables in Midrash* (Cambridge, Mass., 1991), p. 323, note 11.

73. It is reasonable to suppose that Jesus was connected with the legacy of the Qumranic Messiah when he came in contact with John the Baptist. John the Baptist's close relationship with the Qumran community in general lies outside the scope of our present discussion; I hope to deal with it elsewhere. For the present, see the following studies: W. H. Brownlee, "John the Baptist," pp. 33–53; D. R. Schwartz, "On Quirinius, John the Baptist, the Benedictus, Melchizedek, Qumran and Ephesus," *RQ* 13 (1988), pp. 635–46; H. Lichtenberger, "The Dead Sea Scrolls and John the Baptist," in *The Dead Sea Scrolls: Forty Years of Research*, ed. D. Dimant and U. Rappaport (Leiden, 1992), pp. 340–46. Doubts about the connection between John and the Qumran sect have been expressed by J. E. Taylor, *The Immerser: John the Baptist within Second Temple Judaism* (Grand Rapids, 1997), pp. 15–48.

74. Mark 8:27–31. There are parallel traditions in Matthew 16:13–21 and Luke 9:18–22.

75. Bultmann, *Theology of the New Testament*, vol. 1, p. 26.

76. Ibid., vol. 1, p. 31.

77. Vermes, *Jesus the Jew*, p. 38.

78. Similarly, it is written in the Book of Revelation (11:11) that the two prophet-Messiahs were resurrected after three and a half days. The number three and a half was based on Daniel 7:25. For that reason the formula in Hystaspes must be regarded as the original one.

79. We need not enter here into the debate about the difference between the version in Mark 8:31, "after the third day," and the more regular version, "on the third day" (Matthew 16:21; Luke 9:22). Some scholars argue that both versions have essentially the same meaning

(see C. H. Turner, "The Gospel according to St. Mark,"in *A New Commentary on Holy Scripture*, ed. C. Gore, H. L. Goude, and A. Guillaume [London, 1928], vol. 1, pp. 79–80; N. Walker, "After Three Days," *NT* 4 [1960], pp. 261–62, and many others). Others (see H. K. McArthur, "On the Third Day," *NTS* 18 [1971–72], pp. 81–86; M. Smith, *Clement of Alexandria* [Cambridge, Mass., 1973], p. 163, note 8; H. Koester, *Ancient Christian Gospels* [London, 1990], p. 280, note 2) try to find an explanation for the formula in Mark 8:31, which appears to contradict the reports of the resurrection of Jesus on the third day (Matthew 28:1–7; Mark 15:42–16:7; Luke 23:54–24:7). In light of our study we might suggest that the reading of Mark 8:31 reflects the original saying of Jesus, which was based on belief in the resurrection of the Qumranic Messiah "after the third day." (The same reading, "after the third day," is found also in Matthew 27:63 and, in several manuscripts, also in Mark 9:31 and 10:34. See C. Williams, *Alternations to the Texts of the Synoptic Gospels and Acts* [Oxford, 1951], p. 45; B. M. Metzger, *A Textual Commentary on the Greek New Testament* [London, 1975], p. 107; idem, *The Text of the New Testament* [Oxford, 1992], p. 199.)

80. See also Matthew 26:36–44 and Luke 22:41–44.

CHAPTER 3. ANOTHER PARACLETE

1. On the sources concerning the Essenes and their connection with the Qumran literature, see A. Dupont Sommer, *The Essene Writings from Qumran* (Cleveland, 1962), pp. 21–67; F. M. Cross, *The Ancient Library of Qumran* (London, 1958), pp. 52–79. For a summary of the parallels between Josephus's account of the Essene practices and the instructions in the Qumran literature, see J. Baumgarten, "The Disqualification of Priests in 4Q Fragments in the Damascus Document," in *The Madrid Qumran Congress*, ed. J. Trebolle Barrera and L. Vegas Montaner (Leiden, 1992), pp. 504–5. The identification of the Qumran sect with the Essenes is accepted by most scholars of the subject, but at the same time there are some who disagree. Schiffman, for example, regards the people

of Qumran as an extreme branch of the Sadducees. See L. H. Schiffman, *Reclaiming the Dead Sea Scrolls* (Philadelphia, 1994), pp. 75–76, 88–89.

2. 4QHe is the same as 4Q471b. See E. Eshel, "The 'Speaker,'" p. 620, line 6.

3. 4Q491 frg. 11, col. 1. See E. Eshel, "The 'Speaker,'" p. 621–22, line 11.

4. See chapter 1, note 43.

5. In the Bible the phrase refers to an earthly king (1 Chronicles 27:33). Several people are described in the Bible as God's beloved. See Deuteronomy 33:12; 2 Samuel 12:25; Isaiah 41:8.

6. The angels are sometimes described as sons of God (see, for example, Genesis 6:2, Psalm 29:1). Nowhere in the Bible, however, are they described as the king's sons.

7. See Eshel, "The 'Speaker,'" p. 621, line 10.

8. On the "friends" in the courts of Hellenistic rulers, see Ch. Habicht, "Die herrschende Gesellschaft in den Hellenistichen Monarchen," *Vierteljahresschrift für Social und Wirtschaftgeschichte* 45 (1958), p. 1ff. On the "friends" in Herod's court, see A. Schalit, *King Herod* (Jerusalem, 1960), pp. 208–9 (Hebrew).

9. Josephus, *Jewish War* 1.460.

10. See Josephus, *Jewish Antiquities* 15.228; *Jewish War* 1.538, 571, 620. On Herod's courts of law, see Rabello, "*Hausgericht* in the House of Herod the Great?" pp. 119–35.

11. Josephus, *Jewish Antiquities* 15.372–79.

12. See Josephus, *Jewish Antiquities* 13.311–13; idem, *Jewish War* 1.78–80; idem, *Jewish Antiquities* 17.345–48; idem, *Jewish War* 2.111.

13. See Schalit, *King Herod*, pp. 228, 297, 334. On the possible source of this story, see Tal Ilan, "King David, King Herod and Nicolaus of Damascus" *JSQ* 5 (1998) pp. 225–28.

14. See M. Stern, "Herod and the Herodian Dynasty," in *The Jewish People in the First Century*, ed. S. Safrai and M. Stern (Assen, 1974), pp. 270–77; idem, "Social Realignments in Herodian Judea," in *The Jerusalem Cathedra* (Jerusalem, 1982), pp. 40–62.

15. See B. J. Capper, "'With the Oldest Monks' . . . Light from Essene History on the Career of the Beloved Disciple?" *JTS* 49 (1998), pp. 28–29.

16. See E. Schuller, "A Hymn," pp. 610–11, lines 1–5.

17. 1QS 9:21–23.

18. Ibid.

19. See D. Flusser, "Hillel and Jesus: Two Ways of Self-Awareness," in *Hillel and Jesus*, ed. J. H. Charlesworth and L. L. Johns (Minneapolis, 1997), pp. 78–82. On the militant messianism in Qumranic writings of the Herodian period, see K. Atkinson, "On the Herodian Origin of Militant Davidic Messianism at Qumran," *JBL* 118 (1999), pp. 435–60.

20. Mishna, Hagiga 2:2.

21. Scholars disagree about whether there really was a leadership in pairs at that period or whether the account in the Mishna is merely a projection of the conditions of the Tannaic period onto the Second Temple period. See Goodblatt, *Monarchic Principle*, pp. 72–73. Goodblatt claims that in Second Temple times there was no such thing as a leadership in pairs and that this Mishna represents an attempt on the part of second-century rabbis to create a picture of the leadership in the Second Temple period in accordance with the realities of their own time. For the purposes of the present study, however, there is no need to decide about the historicity of leadership in pairs. From our point of view the importance of this Mishna lies in the statement that Menahem "went out." Even if we accept Goodblatt's view, this does not affect the authenticity of the tradition where Menachem's "exit" is concerned. On the other hand, it is hard to believe that anyone in the second century would invent such a story. It undoubtedly reflects a historical event.

22. Mishna, Avot 1:1–12.

23. See J. M. Baumgarten, *Studies in Qumran Law* (Leiden, 1977), p. 10, note 18.

24. See A. Zacuti, *Sefer Yuhasin Shalem*, ed. H. Filipowski (Jerusalem, 1962), pp. 17, 73. Among the scholars who have supported this identification are Azariah De Rossi in his work *Me'or Einayim* (see Rob-

ert Bonfils, *Azaria De Rossi: Selected Chapters from "Sefer Me'or Einayim"* [Jerusalem, 1991], p. 241); H. Graetz, *History of the Jews*, trans. Shaul Pinhas Rabinovitz (Jerusalem, 1972), p. 495 (Hebrew); H. Schorr, *Hehalutz* 7 (1864), p. 60; Joseph Derenbourg, *Essai sur l'histoire et la Géographie de la Palestine* (Paris, 1867), p. 464; and Ch. Albeck, *Mishna Seder Mo'ed* (Jerusalem, 1951), p. 11 (Hebrew).

25. In the Babylonian Talmud, Hagiga 16b, it is said that Menahem "left to do the king's business." This statement should be compared with Daniel 8:27: "I went about the king's business." According to the story in the Bible, Daniel was a member of the court of the king of Babylon.

26. This is the formulation in the Leiden manuscript of the Jerusalem Talmud and in the Venice edition. The confused forms תריהו, חורין appear in quotations of this passage by Rabbi Nissim Gaon (see Nissim Gaon, *Liblli Quinque*, ed. S. Abramson ([Jerusalem 1965], p. 70) and the commentary on the Mishna by Rabbi Nathan (*Kirjat Sepher* 10, ed. S. Assaf [1935], p. 541). On the other hand, in the extracts from Rabbi Nissim Gaon's book that are published in J. N. Epstein's *Studies in Talmudic Literature and Semitic Languages* (Jerusalem, 1988), vol. 2, p. 268, the formulation is תריסי. This form appears to be a scholarly correction by someone who knew that the rare word תירקי means "armor" in Greek and replaced it with the more common תריסי, "shields." In the Babylonian Talmud, however, תירקי was changed to סיריקין, "silken garments," in accordance with the description of Menahem in the Babylonian Talmud as someone who "left to do the king's business." On the versions in the Midrash to the Song of Songs Zuta, see S. Lieberman, *Greek in Jewish Palestine* (New York, 1965), p. 181, note 187. As Lieberman and Alon realized (G. Alon, *Jews, Judaism and the Classical World* [Jerusalem, 1977], pp. 332–33), a comparison of the various versions reveals that the original form was תירקי. The changes and confusions were due to the fact that the word תירקי is a rare one in the literature of the Sages, and was therefore not understood correctly.

27. On תירקי, "coats of armor," see Alon, *Jews, Judaism and the Classical World*; Lieberman, *Greek in Jewish Palestine*; and A. Tal, "תרקיה," in

Studies in Rabbinic Literature, Bible and Jewish History, ed. Y. D. Gilat, Ch. Levine, and Z. M. Rabinowitz (Ramat Gan, 1982), pp. 256–60 (Hebrew).

28. Jerusalem Talmud, Hagiga 2:2 (77b).

29. This tradition does not date from later than the second century CE. This is shown by the fact that in the Beraita in the Babylonian Talmud תירקי has already changed to סיריקין. The Baraita is a Tannaic source that dates from no later than the first half of the third century. It therefore follows that the date of the tradition in the Jerusalem Talmud can be no later than the second century.

30. On the display of shining weapons as a symbol of success in battle, see D. Gera, "The Battle of Beth Zacharia and Greek Literature," in *The Jews in the Hellenistic-Roman World: Studies in Memory of Menahem Stern*, ed. I. M. Gafni, A. Oppenheimer, and D. R. Schwartz (Jerusalem, 1996), pp. 27–31 (Hebrew).

31. "Write on a bull's horns" is the formula ascribed in the Midrash to a decree of Antiochus Epiphanes (see Midrash, Bereshit Rabba 2:4, ed. J. Theodor and Ch. Albeck, p. 11 and parallels). This expression was perhaps intended as an ironical comment on the expression of Menahem's followers, "to raise up the horn of the Messiah"—referring to Menahem.

32. The expression "eighty pairs" corresponds to the size of a military unit and is probably figurative. See B. Z. Luria, "Who is Menahem?" *Sinai* 55 (1964), pp. 300–301 (Hebrew). Lieberman *(Greek in Jewish Palestine)* in note 186 declares himself in agreement with the opinion of J. Derenbourg *(Essai sur l'Histoire et la Géographie de la Palestine*, p. 464), that the Menahem who "went out" with his disciples clad in shining armor was Menahem the Galilean, the leader of the *sicarii*— the Zealots—at the time of the Jewish War, and not the Menahem who was Hillel's counterpart. But although the Midrash to the Song of Songs Zuta combines these two personalities, there is no hint of any such combination in the Jerusalem Talmud. There is no reason to suppose that the tradition in the Jerusalem Talmud does not relate solely to the

Menahem who was Hillel's contemporary. The sayings about Menahem in both Talmuds—"He left to do the king's business," "He went forth into evil courses," "He went from one way of behaving to another"—fit very well with what we know about the Menahem who was Hillel's contemporary, but they don't fit Menahem the Sicarii.

33. See G. Scholem, *Jewish Gnosticism, Merkaba Mysticism, and Talmudic Tradition* (New York, 1960).

34. See the attempt to solve this problem in Maimonides' commentary on the Mishna. The associative connection between the word עריות in the Mishna at the end of chapter 1 of Hagiga and in the Mishna at the beginning of chapter 2 is not sufficient reason for inserting a discussion of this prohibition in the tractate Hagiga.

35. On the use of the verb יצא, "go out," as a term for turning heretic, see S. Lieberman, *Studies in Palestinian Talmudic Literature* (Jerusalem, 1991), p. 281, note 1 (Hebrew).

36. Talmud Babli, Hagiga 16b. As Ch. Albeck noted, this section of the tractate Hagiga contains further references to turning heretic. See Ch. Albeck, *A Commentary to the Mishna* (Jerusalem, 1952), vol. 2, p. 393 (Hebrew). The same expression "He went forth into evil courses" is used in Talmud Babli, Hagigah 15a regarding Elisha—*aher*. It seems to me that the heresy of Elisha was connected with the figure of Menahem. Elisha's title *aher* is to be explained in relation to the expression *derech aheret* (literally: different way, heterodoxy), which is the common title for the Qumran sect in Rabbinic literature; see S. Lieberman, *Texts and Studies* (New York, 1974), pp. 190–99.

37. See Baumgarten, *Studies in Qumran Law*, pp. 68, 73; and E. and H. Eshel, "4Q471 Fragment 1 and Ma'amadot in the War Scroll," in *The Madrid Qumran Congress*, ed. J. Trebolle Barrera and L. Vegas Montaner (Leiden, 1992), pp. 611–20.

38. Midrash, Song of Songs Zuta 8:14, S. Buber edition (Wilno, 1925), p. 38. The reference to the dispute between Menahem and Hillel is in contradiction to the statement of the Mishna in the tractate Hagiga that "Hillel and Menahem were not in disagreement." If this was so,

Hillel and Menahem did not disagree about the laying of hands on sacrifices, but they were in disagreement about Menahem's messianic claims.

39. Despite the historical confusion that appears in the continuation of the Midrash to the Song of Songs Zuta (see note 32, this chapter), there is no reason to doubt the authenticity of the statement about the dispute between Menahem and Hillel.

40. Tosefta, Sukkah 4:3; and see the comments and interpretation in Flusser, *Judaism*, pp. 511–12.

41. Leviticus Rabba 1:5, ed. M. Margulies (Jerusalem, 1958), pp. 17–18. See Flusser's comments in *Judaism*, pp. 512–13.

42. Scholem, *Messianic Idea*, pp. 89–90.

43. Avot de Rabbi Nathan, version b, chapter 30, ed. S. Z. Schechter (Vienna, 1847), p. 66; and Leviticus Rabba 34:3 (ed. Margulies, p. 777).

44. 4Q491 frg. 11, col. 1:7.

45. See I. Knohl, "A Parasha Concerned with Accepting the Kingdom of Heaven," *Tarbiz* 53 (1983), pp. 23–24 (Hebrew).

46. See Flusser, *Judaism*, p. 513.

47. See M. Stern, "Herod and the Herodian Dynasty," in *The Jewish People in the First Century*, ed. S. Safrai and M. Stern (Assen, 1974), pp. 240–41.

48. Hillel's view had a decisive influence on the thinking and the law of the following generations. See Y. Lorberbaum, *Imago Dei: Rabbinic Literature, Maimonides and Nachmanides* (Ph.D. diss., Hebrew University, Jerusalem, 1997).

49. See Josephus, *Jewish Antiquities* 17.298, as well as the statement in 17.339 about the accusation made against the High Priest Joezer, son of Boethus, that he had befriended the rebels.

50. Stern, "Herod and the Herodian Dynasty," p. 280. The fact that Menahem is not mentioned by Josephus as one of the leaders of the revolt does not invalidate the information given in rabbinic sources about Menahem's military activities. Moreover, Josephus himself said that there were other leaders besides those he mentioned (*Jewish Antiquities* 7:285). Perhaps the omission of Menahem's name was motivated by

Josephus's desire not to spoil the picture he was trying to paint of the Essenes as a peace-loving group.

51. Josephus, *Jewish Antiquities* 17.149–67.

52. For a detailed account of the revolt, see E. Schürer, *The History of the Jewish People in the Age of Jesus Christ*, rev. and ed. G. Vermes and F. Millar (Edinburgh, 1973), vol. 1, pp. 330–35; E. M. Smallwood, *The Jews under Roman Rule* (Leiden, 1976), pp. 105–10; and E. Paltiel, "War in Judea after Herod's Death," *RBPH* 59 (1981), pp. 107–36.

53. Josephus, *Jewish Antiquities* 17. 254–64; idem, *Jewish War* 2.42–50.

54. We cannot know at exactly what stage of the revolt the messianic leaders were killed.

55. John 14:16–17, 26; 15:26; 16:13.

56. John 16:8–11.

57. John 16:7.

58. See R. Bultmann, *The Gospel of John* (Oxford, 1971), p. 567 and note 1; Behm, s.v. "παράκλητος," *TDOT* 5, 1967, p. 800, note 1; R. E. Brown, "The Paraclete in the Fourth Gospel," *NTS* 13 (1966–67), p. 114, note 1.

59. See P. J. Kobelski, "Melchizedek and Melchiresa," *CBQMS* 10 (Washington, 1981), pp. 100–103; and the discussion in Behm, s.v. "παράκλητος," pp. 800–803.

60. Bultmann, *Gospel of John*, p. 570.

61. See Behm, pp. 801–2, and J. G. Davis, "The Primary Meaning of 'ΠΑΡΑΚΛΗΤΟΣ,'" *JTS* n.s. 4 (1953), pp. 35–38.

62. O. Betz, *Der Paraclet* (Leiden, 1963), p. 140; Kobelski, "Melchizedek and Melchiresa," p. 104; Behm, p. 805.

63. Bultmann, *Gospel of John*, pp. 569–70.

64. Ibid., pp. 570–72.

65. See the criticisms of Behm, s.v. "παράκλητος," pp. 807–9, and Brown, "Paraclete in the Fourth Gospel," p. 119.

66. See the survey of the scholarship on this subject in Kobelski, "Melchizedek and Melchiresa," pp. 105–7.

67. See 1QS 3:13–4:14.

68. See Cross, *Ancient Library of Qumran*, pp. 157–61; Betz, *Der Paraclet*, pp. 64–69, 137–75; Brown, "Paraclete in the Fourth Gospel," p. 118; Kobelski, "Melchizedek and Melchiresa," pp. 106–14; A. R. C. Leaney, "The Johannine Paraclete and the Qumran Scrolls," in *John and Qumran*, ed. J. H. Charlesworth (London, 1972), pp. 38ff.

69. See note 63, this chapter.

70. The idea that "Paraclete" is a translation of the Hebrew personal name *Menahem* has already been suggested by A. Geiger and H. Gressmann. However, they were thinking about Menahem the leader of the Zealots in 66 CE. See H. Gressmann, *Der Messias* (Göttingen, 1929), pp. 460–61.

71. The symbolic significance of the name, expressing the consolation that would come with the appearance of the Messiah, undoubtedly also played a role here.

72. See Babylonian Talmud, Sanhedrin 98b; Jerusalem Talmud, Brachot 2:5, 5:1; Lamentations Rabba 1:16, S. Buber edition (Wilno, 1899), p. 88; Lamentations Midrash Zuta, S. Buber edition (Wilno, 1899), p. 73; L. Grünhut, *Yalkut of R. Machir Bar Abba Mari on Proverbs* (Jerusalem, 1967), p. 103.

73. John 14:16, and see note 60, this chapter.

74. Bultmann, *Gospel of John*, pp. 566–67; Brown, "Paraclete in the Fourth Gospel," pp. 126–27; and Kobelski, "Melchizedek and Melchiresa," p. 105.

75. Bultmann, *Gospel of John*, p. 567.

76. Of note in this connection is the recent suggestion that the Gospel of John may have been written under the influence of Essene circles in Jerusalem. See B. J. Capper, "With the Oldest Monks . . . ," *JTS* 49 (1998), pp. 1–55.

77. See the recent discussion of this subject in Capper (ibid., pp. 36–42).

78. Capper suggested that the upper room was owned by the

"beloved disciple," who belonged to the Essene community in Jerusalem.

POSTSCRIPT

1. In the original version the mother uses the expression "Israel's foe" to refer to her son. This is to avoid saying directly, "I would like to strangle my son."

2. The story as given here is translated from the Aramaic of the Jerusalem Talmud, Brachot 2:4, 5a. There is a parallel tradition in Lamentations Rabba 1:16, S. Buber edition (Wilno, 1899), p. 89. See also the versions in Lamentations Zuta, S. Buber edition, p. 73, and in the supplement to *Yalkut of R. Machir Bar Abba Mari on Proverbs*, ed. L. Grünhut, 103b.

3. The name may contain a reference to the family of freedom fighters from Galilee who led the rebellion against the Romans. On this family, see M. Stern, *Studies in Jewish History*. On the resemblance between Menahem, son of Hezekiah, in the story and in the family of freedom-fighters, see L. Ginzberg, *A Commentary on the Palestinian Talmud*, vol. 1 (New York, 1971), p. 339 (Hebrew).

4. In describing this event, the Talmud uses the rare word עלעולין to denote the wind that carried Menahem away. Frenkel observes that this word is used in the Aramaic translation of 2 Kings 11 to describe the ascension of Elijah (J. Frenkel, *Studies in the Spiritual World of the Agadic Story* [Tel Aviv, 1981], p. 163, note 19 [Hebrew]).

5. G. Hasan-Rokem, *The Web of Life* (Tel Aviv, 1996), pp. 165–66 (Hebrew).

6. Matthew 2:1–10, and see the discussion in R. E. Brown, *The Birth of the Messiah* (New York, 1977).

7. This was pointed out by Hasan-Rokem in *Web of Life*, pp. 165–67.

8. Ibid.

9. One must point out, in this connection, the traditions that say

that the name of the Messiah is "Menahem." See Babylonian Talmud, Sanhedrin 98b; Jerusalem Talmud 2:4, 5a; Lamentations Rabba 1:16.

10. Beraita, Babylonian Talmud, Sukkah 52a. See the collection of later talmudic sources and the translations in Y. Heinemann's article, "The Messiah, Son of Ephraim and the Exodus from Egypt of the Sons of Ephraim before the End," *Tarbiz* 40 (1971), p. 450 (Hebrew). To the bibliographical information given there in note 1, one should add C. C. Torrey, "The Messiah, Son of Ephraim," *JBL* 66 (1947), pp. 268–72; and Y. Liebes, "Yonah Ben Amitai as Messiah the Son of Joseph," *Studies in Cabbala and Philosophy Presented to L. Tishbi on His Seventy-Fifth Birthday* (Jerusalem, 1986), pp. 269–311 (Hebrew).

11. See, in detail, I. Knohl, "On the 'Son of God,' Armillus and Messiah, the Son of Joseph," *Tarbiz* 68 (1998), pp. 13–38 (Hebrew).

APPENDIX A: THE MESSIANIC HYMNS

1. The main assessment of the relationship between the two versions of the first hymn is to be found in J. J. Collins and D. Dimant, "A Thrice-Told Hymn," in *JQR* 85 (1994), pp. 151–55; and in D. Dimant, "A Synoptic Comparison of Parallel Sections in 4Q427 7, 4Q491 11 and 4Q471b," in *JQR* 85 (1994), pp. 157–161. A further discussion of the subject is to be found in E. Eshel, "4Q471b: A Self-Glorification Hymn," *RQ* 17 (1996), pp. 175–203.

2. The version of the fragments given here is from Eshel, "The 'Speaker'"; also in idem, "471b: 4Q Self-Glorification Hymn," pp. 427–28. Eshel published this manuscript as 4Q471b, although she agrees that all these fragments belong to the manuscript that contains the fragment known as 4QHe. I prefer to regard all these fragments as belonging with 4QHe, as does Eileen Schuller in her edition of the thanksgiving psalms from cave 4, published in *DJD* 29 ("431: 4Q Hodayot").

3. Eshel completed the letters תחש as א]תחש[ב.

4. Generally speaking, the reconstruction proposed here is based on

the one in Eshel's article ("The 'Speaker'"). I have deviated from her reconstruction in a few places, which I shall indicate in these notes.

5. The reconstruction is according to 4Q491 frg. 11, col. 1:7.

6. The reading and reconstruction חדל [אישים] was suggested by Eshel in her article ("The 'Speaker'"). E. Schuller ("431: 4Q Hodayot," pp. 203–5) thinks that the two fragments are consecutive, and she reconstructs the phrase as וחדל [ה]רע. Eshel's reconstruction seems to me preferable to Schuller's because the writer's use of the expression נבזה כמוני makes it seems likely that he was influenced here by Isaiah 53:3: נבזה וחדל אישים. Schuller's suggestion that the expression חדלהרע should be translated "lacking of/without companion" is unconvincing. Schuller also suggests two other possible translations of the expression: (1) "evil ceases" and (2) "he ceased from evil"; but these suggestions do not suit the character of the hymn, which is written in the first person. Furthermore, evidence is not sufficient that these two fragments should be regarded as consecutive; therefore, one should allow a textual space between them, as Eshel does. Schuller claims that a comparison with the fragments of the hymn in 4QHa frg. 7, col. 1:6–8, shows that the fragments have to be regarded as consecutive, but the incompleteness of these fragments and the differences in the various manuscripts of the hymn and within the very same version weaken her argument.

7. The phrase was reconstructed in accordance with line 9 of 4Q491 frg. 11, col. 1.

8. Ibid., line 6.

9. Ibid., line 10.

10. Ibid.

11. The reconstruction "the beloved of the king, a companion of the ho[ly ones. And none can . . . and to my glory]" is according to 4QHa frg. 7, col. 1:10, in Schuller's rendering in *DJD* 29 ("427: 4Q Hodayot," p. 96).

12. See 4QHa frg. 7, col. 1:12–13; 4Q491 frg. 11, col. 1:18.

13. The preceding lines contain the remnant of another hymn, which is in praise of God and is written in the third person.

14. The reconstruction of the text is that made by Eshel in her article "4Q471b: A Self-Glorification Hymn," p. 184.

15. The translation given here is according to that of E. Schuller in "427: 4Q Hodayot," pp. 99–100. Schuller's reconstructions of the text are partly based on parallel formulations in 4QHe and 1QHa. The reconstructions that are based on those parallels are underlined.

16. Following the conclusion "Let them say: blessed is God . . . to all the children of his truth" (lines 12–14), there is another hymn, beginning, "We have known you, O God of righteousness." (In 1QHa frg. 7, this hymn also appears immediately after the second hymn.) It would seem that this hymn does not form part of our composition but belongs to the original text of the Thanksgivings Scroll. In this hymn we find the usual worldview of the Thanksgivings, stressing human beings' existential guilt for being merely creatures of flesh and blood: "What is flesh in relation to these things and how shall it be reckoned?" This guilt is atoned for by God's "abundant mercies and marvelous forgiveness." In contrast, as J. J. Collins rightly points out (*Scepter and the Star*, p. 148), the sense of existential guilt is entirely absent from the messianic hymns. Rather, there is a sense of total liberation from sin (" כלה עוון "), a feeling appropriate to the eschatological atmosphere depicted here. The linguistic similarity between the conclusion of the second messianic hymn ("so that they might know the abundance of his loving kindnesses") and the beginning of the hymn that follows ("We have known you, O God of righteousness") may be a literary device to make the messianic hymns blend more easily with the original text of the Thanksgivings Scroll. This device was no doubt intended to confer on the messianic hymns some of the authority of the Thanksgivings, and this may also have had liturgical consequences.

17. The reconstruction is that of Eshel, "4Q471b: A Self-Glorification Hymn," p. 184. For the translation of line 15, see note 55 in chapter 1.

18. 4Q491 frg. 11, col. 1:15. In the manuscript, the formulation is

[ ]מש. The last letter could be ש or ע. The reconstruction מש[יחו] was proposed by Dimant ("A Synoptic Comparison," p. 159).

19. Baillet, *DJD* 7, pp. 26–29.

20. M. Smith, "Ascent to the Heavens and Deification in 4QMa," in *Archaeology and History in the Dead Sea Scrolls*, ed. L. Schiffman (Sheffield, 1990), pp. 186–88; idem, "Two Ascended to Heaven—Jesus and the Author of 4Q491," in *Jesus and the Dead Sea Scrolls*, ed. J. H. Charlesworth (New York, 1992), pp. 290–301.

21. See also Dimant, "A Synoptic Comparison," p. 161.

22. J. J. Collins, "A Throne in the Heavens: Apotheosis in Pre-Christian Judaism," in *Death, Ecstasy, and Other-Worldly Journeys*, ed. J. J. Collins and M. Fishbane (New York, 1995), p. 55.

23. Collins, *Scepter and the Star*, p. 148.

24. Collins, *Apocalypticism*, p. 147.

25. Ibid., p. 146.

26. This possibility was suggested by Abegg. See M. G. Abegg, "Who Ascended to Heaven? 4Q491, 4Q427 and the Teacher of Righteousness."

27. This idea was put forward by Stegemann and Steudel. See A. Steudel, "The Eternal Reign of the People of God," *RQ* 17 (1966), p. 525, note 93; H. Stegemann, "Some Remarks to 1QSa, to 1QSb, and to Qumran Messianism," *RQ* 17 (1966), pp. 497–505.

28. Collins, *Apocalypticism*, p. 147.

29. Ibid.

30. Eshel, "4Q471b: A Self-Glorification Hymn," pp. 191–98; and idem, "The 'Speaker,'" pp. 631–33.

31. 1QSb, col. 4:24–28.

32. For a discussion of the various suggestions concerning the identity of the receiver of the blessing, see Eshel, "The 'Speaker,'" pp. 631–33.

33. 1QSb, col. 4:24–28.

34. See "No teaching compares to my teaching" in the hymn.

35. See, for example, Exodus 28:35 and 43, 29:30, 30:20; Deuteronomy 10:8, 18:7, 21:5; Ezekiel 44:15, etc.

36. See Exodus 39:30; Leviticus 8:9.

37. For descriptions of the angels standing before God, who sits on his throne, see 1 Kings 22:19 and Isaiah 6:1–2. See also Zechariah 3:7; Job 1:6.

38. See 2 Samuel 12:25; 1 Chronicles 29:23.

39. 4QHe frg. 1–2.

40. 4Q491 frg. 11, col. 1:9.

41. As Stegemann and Steudel suggested (see note 27, this chapter).

42. 4QHa frg. 7, col. 2:8–10.

43. 1QHa 11:22–23.

44. 4QHa frg. 7, col. 2:5, 6.

45. 4QHa frg. 7, col. 1:13, 14.

46. See also 1QHa 12:14–18; J. Licht, *The Thanksgiving Scroll* (Jerusalem, 1957), p. 175.

47. The general character of the messianic hymn as a description of the present shows that one is not dealing here with the prophetic past.

APPENDIX B:
BETWEEN ROME AND JERUSALEM

1. Mark 15:39; Matthew 27:54. See T. H. Kim, "The Anarthrous υἱὸς θεοῦ in Mark 15.39 and the Roman Imperial Cult," *Biblica* 79 (1998), pp. 221–41.

2. Bultmann, *History of the Synoptic Tradition*, p. 291 and note 4.

3. The document is known as 4Q246, officially published in E. Puech, "4Q apocryphe de Daniel ar," *DJD* 17 (Oxford, 1996), pp. 165–84. See also the bibliographical lists in Puech, note 1; and F. Garcia Martinez, "The Messianic Figures in the Qumran Texts," in *Current Research and Technological Developments in the Study of the Dead Sea Scrolls*, ed. D. W. Parry and S. R. Ricks (Leiden, 1996), p. 25, note 16. In the same collection of articles, see also F. M. Cross, "Notes on the Doctrine of the Two Messiahs at Qumran." One should also note some other articles that have appeared recently: E. M. Cook, "4Q246," *BBR* 5 (1995), pp. 43–66;

J. J. Collins, "The Background of the 'Son of God' Text," *BBR* 7 (1997), pp. 51–61; E. Puech, "Some Remarks on 4Q246 and 4Q521 and Qumran Messianism," in *The Provo Conference on the Dead Sea Scrolls*, ed. D. W. Parry and E. Ulrich (Leiden, 1999), pp. 545–65; A. Steudel, "The Eternal Reign of the People of God," *RQ* 17 (1996), pp. 514–16; and J. Zimmerman, "Observations on 4Q246—The 'Son of God,'" in *Qumran Messianism*, ed. J. A. Charlesworth et al (Tübingen, 1998), pp. 175–90.

4. Unless otherwise noted, the translation of the texts and the reconstruction are taken from Puech, "4Q apocryphe de Daniel ar," p. 547.

5. I followed here the translation by Cross ("Notes on the Doctrine of the Two Messiahs," p. 7). Puech translates here: "and by this name he will be designated."

6. Cross translates this: "like comets that you saw (in your vision)"; Puech translates it: "like the meteors of the vision."

7. Vacat means an empty line or half line in the original text. This is a way to sign the beginning of a new issue.

8. Because of the structural similarity between this document and Daniel chapter 7, Milik came to the conclusion that the "son of God" was the wicked king who would be succeeded by the "people of God." See J. T. Milik, "Les modeles arameens du livre d'Esther dans la Grotte 4 de Qumran," *RQ* 15 (1992), pp. 383–84. E. Puech, who put out the document as part of the official publication of the Qumran literature, has recently declared himself in agreement with this view (see Puech, "Some Remarks"). Milik and Puech thought that the figure described here was a historical personage. Milik suggested that it was the Seleucid monarch Alexander Balas (150–145 BCE), who called himself the "son of God." I find this suggestion difficult: The "son of God" is described in this text as a king who will be great on earth; all kings will make peace with him and will serve him. This description dose not fit the historical figure of Alexander Balas, who was not a great king ruling over the earth and was not served by all. Puech and Steudel (see note 3, this chapter) suggested identifying the "son of God" with Antiochus IV. However,

Antiochus IV was not called the "son of God." Other scholars object to the identification of the "Son of God" with a wicked king. Is it possible, they ask, that exalted titles like "son of God" and "son of the Most High" could apply to a wicked king and, if so, how is it that these titles are used in the Gospel of Luke to describe the figure of Jesus? These scholars consequently conclude that the "son of God" in the Qumran document must be a positive messianic figure. (See the articles by Cross and Collins mentioned in note 3, this chapter.) The problem with this view was correctly pointed out by Puech and Steudel: An understanding of the "son of God" figure as a positive messianic figure is connected with the division of the text into four units: I 4–6, I 7–II 1a, II 1b–3, II 4–9. However, the text is divided by the *vacat* (space) into two units only, and there is no evidence for additional division in II 1.

9. Puech, "4Q apocryphe de Daniel ar," p. 166.

10. That was the opinion of Milik, for instance, who identified the "son of God" with one of the Seleucid monarchs.

11. Pliny, *Natural History*, trans. H. Rackham (Cambridge: Harvard University Press, 1958). See Suetonius, "Iulius," 88, in *The Lives of the Caesars;* Dio Cassius, *Roman History* 45.7.1; Servius on Virgil, *Eclogues* 9.46.

12. On the "golden age" and Augustus, see K. Galinski, *Augustan Culture* (Princeton, 1996), p. 91 ff.

13. On the comet and its significance, see Taylor, *Divinity of the Roman Emperor*, pp. 90–92, 112–14; Weinstock, *Divus Julius*, pp. 370–84; Fishwick, *The Imperial Cult*, p. 74; and P. Zanker, *The Power of Images in the Age of Augustus* (Ann Arbor, 1988), pp. 34–35.

14. See Taylor, *Divinity of the Roman Emperor*, p. 106; and Fishwick, *The Imperial Cult*, p. 76. Octavian began to use this title around 40 BCE.

15. See Daniel 7:23. This view of Rome as the fourth beast, which tramples the whole earth, is in agreement with the description of the Romans in the Pesher Habakkuk found in Qumran:

[W]ho trample the earth with their horses and with their beasts. And from a distance they come, from the islands of the sea, to

devour all the peoples like an eagle, and there is no satiety . . .
they divide up their yoke and their forced service—their food—
upon all the peoples year by year to lay waste many lands.
(Pesher Habakkuk 3:9–12, 6:6–8)

16. Suetonius, "Augustus," 94.

17. See the description of Augustus as the redeemer of humanity in Philo's *De Legatione ad Gaium*, 143–47.

18. Bultmann, *History of the Synoptic Tradition*, p. 291 and note 4.

19. According to Brown, Augustus was mentioned in Luke (2:1) in order to assert that Jesus, not Augustus, was the true redeemer who would bring peace to the world. See Brown, *Birth of the Messiah*, pp. 415–16.

20. For a bibliography on the "Fourth Eclogue," see W. W. Briggs, "A Bibliography of Virgil's Eclogues," *ANRW* II 31.2 (1981), 1311–25.

21. Virgil, Fourth Eclogue 1–14, trans. H. Rushton Fairclough (Cambridge, Mass., 1942). The vision of the "end of days" in Isaiah 11:6–8 is recalled in the way Virgil describes the "new age":

Uncalled, the goats shall bring home their udders swollen with
    milk
and the herds shall not fear huge lions. . . . The serpent, too,
    shall perish.

On the possibility of the influence of Jewish sources on Virgil, see R. G. M. Nisbet, "Virgil's Fourth Eclogue: Easterners and Westerners," *BICS* 25 (1978), pp. 59–78. But see also the reservations of J. J. Collins in *Seers, Sybils and Sages in Hellenistic-Roman Judaism* (Leiden, 1997), pp. 194–97.

22. At any rate, according to Schuller's reconstruction.

23. See Virgil, Fourth Eclogue 48; see also the discussion of the subject in T. Frank, *Classical Philology* 11 (1916), pp. 334–36; and W. Tarn, "Helios and the Golden Age," *JRS* 22 (1932), p. 155.

24. Virgil, Fourth Eclogue 15–17, Rushton edition, p. 31.

25. 4Q491 frg. 11, col. 1:6–7; Eshel, "4Q471b: A Self-Glorification Hymn," p. 185.

26. D. A. Slater, "Was the Fourth Eclogue Written to Celebrate the Marriage of Octavia to Mark Anthony?—A Literary Parallel," *CR* 26 (1912), p. 114–19.

27. See W. Clausen, *A Commentary on Virgil's Eclogues* (Oxford, 1994), pp. 121–22.

28. Virgil, *Aeneid* 6.791–93.

29. See Taylor, *Divinity of the Roman Emperor*; K. Galinski, *Augustan Culture*, p. 115.

30. Decision of the Assembly of the Province of Asia, translation adapted from N. Lewis and M. Reinolds, eds., *Roman Civilization* (1955), vol. 2, p. 64.

31. P. Zanker, *Power of Images in the Age of Augustus.*

32. Augustus is depicted sitting in the company of the goddess Roma in Gemma Augusta. A similar scene is depicted on a Ptolemaic cameo of ca. 30–28 BCE. See Galinski, *Augustan Culture*, p. 115. On silver cups from Boscoreale, Augustus is depicted sitting on a royal throne surrounded by gods. See Ann L. Kuttmer, *Dynasty and Empire in the Age of Augustus* (Berkeley, 1995), p. 56ff.

33. 4Q491 frg. 11, col. 1:5; Eshel, "4Q471b: A Self-Glorification Hymn," p. 185.

34. Josephus, *Jewish Antiquities* 14.388.

35. Ibid., 15:343. See note 18, chapter 1.

36. For the possibility of influence of the Imperial Cult in the time of Augustus on Jews of Herod's realm, see A. Yarbro Collins, "The Worship of Jesus and the Imperial Cult," ed. C. Newman et al., in *The Jewish Roots of Christological Monotheism, Supplement to the Journal for the Study of Judaism* 63 (1999), pp. 254–57.

INDEX

Text:	Janson
Display:	Scala Sans
Design:	Barbara Jellow
Index:	Andrew Christenson
Composition:	G & S Typesetters, Inc.
Printing and binding:	Thomson-Shore, Inc.